T0299249

Routledge Revivals

The War Debt and How to Meet It

First published in 1919, this book traces the growth of War Debt during the First World War, examines the real meaning of the Debt and discusses the proposals for clearing it. As the chief contemporary proposal put forward for meeting the interest and repaying the principal of the Debt was the "Conscription of Wealth", or the "Capital Levy", this provides a main focus for the analysis. The author also examines whether the methods of financing war — by borrowing the required money — is sound and whether it should be replaced by taxation. A plan for the reform of income tax is put forward, designed to yield two-thirds of the revenue needed for a Peace Budget that also addresses the War Debt.

The War Debt and How to Meet It

With an Examination of the Proposed "Capital Levy"

J.E. Allen

Routledge
Taylor & Francis Group

First published in 1919
by Methuen & Co. Ltd

This edition first published in 2017 by Routledge
2 Park Square, Milton Park, Abingdon, Oxon, OX14 4RN

and by Routledge
711 Third Avenue, New York, NY 10017

Routledge is an imprint of the Taylor & Francis Group, an informa business

Publisher's Note
The publisher has gone to great lengths to ensure the quality of this
reprint but points out that some imperfections in the original copies may
be apparent.

Disclaimer
The publisher has made every effort to trace copyright holders and
welcomes correspondence from those they have been unable to contact.

A Library of Congress record exists under LC control number: 19009785

ISBN 13: 978-1-138-22325-7 (hbk)
ISBN 13: 978-1-315-40522-3 (ebk)

THE WAR DEBT

AND HOW TO MEET IT

WITH AN EXAMINATION OF THE PROPOSED
"CAPITAL LEVY"

BY

J. E. ALLEN

METHUEN & CO. LTD.
36 ESSEX STREET W.C.
LONDON

First Published in 1919

INTRODUCTION

THE aim of this little book is to trace the growth of the War Debt, to examine the real meaning of the Debt, and to discuss proposals for redeeming it. Since the chief proposal hitherto put forward for meeting the interest and repaying the principal of the Debt is the " Conscription of Wealth " or the " Capital Levy," I have felt bound to deal with this plan at some length. Incidentally, I ask whether the accepted method of financing the war, *i.e.* by borrowing the money required for the wages of munition workers, for the pay of our soldiers, and for the allowances to their dependents, is a sound one. I venture to urge that the money required for these weekly payments, since it is very quickly spent by the recipients, should be obtained by taxation and not by borrowing.

Many of the ideas contained in this book have been gained in my work (since the spring of 1915) as Hon. Secretary of the Committee appointed by the Economic Section of the British Association to report on

v

" The Effects of the War on Credit, Currency and Finance," and of the later Sub-Committee on " Income Tax Reform." But the views expressed here must not be taken as being those of either Committee, though I believe that the Committees, and indeed all economists, are agreed in deploring the financial methods adopted by the Government in the first year of the war.

The after-war burden of taxation must be heavy, but it need not be intolerable if the revenue required is raised by an equitable system of direct taxation, *i.e.* a reformed Income Tax, and not by devices which hamper trade or production. I submit a rough plan for the reform of the Income Tax, designed to make it yield about two-thirds of the revenue needed in a Peace Budget.

I have to acknowledge, with thanks, the permission of the Editor of the *Fortnightly Review* to reprint parts of my articles on " The Conscription of Wealth " and " The War Budgets."

J. E. ALLEN

1 MITRE COURT BUILDINGS,
   TEMPLE, E.C. 4.
   January, 1919.

CONTENTS

THE WAR DEBT

CHAPTER I

THE WAR DEBT

BEFORE considering how the War Debt
should be redeemed we must first see
how it came into being.

When a war begins the Governments of
the belligerent countries at once require the
services of a vast number of men, and, as this
war has shown, of a vast number of women
too. Then they require a corresponding
supply of commodities, food, clothing, ammunition, guns, transport and machinery for
their armed forces.

These requirements mean that the Governments must somehow command the services
of the men and women, and must secure a
constant supply of the commodities. In the
case of the continental nations, and, later in
the conflict, of our own country and the

United States, the Governments obtain the services of the men who are to fight by conscription, *i.e.* these men are compelled to become soldiers on pain of imprisonment or execution.   In addition they obtain pay, which varies from a few pence a day on the Continent to several shillings a day for our colonial troops and our American allies; whilst allowances, also varying in amount, are paid to the soldier's family or dependents. All Governments also claim the right of commandeering any particular goods which they may need, with or without payment, and, more particularly, the right of entering, using and taking, land or houses.

But most of the commodities are only taken in return for payment, sometimes at market prices, sometimes at prices fixed by Government officials. Naturally, the payment made for land and houses depends upon circumstances; in the face of the enemy no landowner or houseowner would ask for rent; but when his property is taken, say in England, where there is no danger from the enemy, he may expect a fair rent. Apparently the Government sometimes relies upon the royal prerogative and does not admit any legal obligation to pay rent ; this contention, however, is so clearly inequitable that we may ignore it, and assume, for economic purposes, that a rent is paid in all cases.

The chief thing which nowadays Government wants in war time is labour. Behind the actual fighting-line there is a second army working on roads and railways, sending up supplies of food and munitions, repairing vehicles, clothing, boots and the other *impedimenta* of an army. Behind them again comes the third army of workers at home who supply all that is needed by armies at the front or on the lines of communication. In no previous war has this third army attained anything like the dimensions or importance of the present. All these millions of workers, or most of them, have to be attracted from other occupations into the war factories and into the offices which manage the enormous clerical work of the war. It might have been possible to secure the services of all these workers by the same means as the services of our fighting-men were obtained, *i.e.* by compulsion, and no logical objection could be taken to such action. Indeed a much stronger case can be made out for *universal* national service in war time than for compulsion applied to one particular kind of service only.

But no kind of compulsion, except the appeal to " do your bit," was applied to war workers ; consequently, in order to attract them in sufficient numbers, exceptionally high wages and salaries were offered. A large part of the work required by the Government is still done in privately-owned factories, and contractors were urged to increase their output and to extend their workshops regardless of expense. So they in turn sought to attract more workers by the offer of high wages. In some cases contractors were not required to submit tenders, but were ordered to carry out certain works and then to charge the actual cost to the Government, taking as their remuneration a percentage on the total cost. Under such conditions, and knowing that speed was of great importance, it was not to be expected that contractors would haggle very long over rates of wages, especially as they obtained an extra percentage for themselves out of each rise in wages. The combined results of all these influences was a steady rise in the rates of wages.

THE FIRST STEP

In normal times the money to pay wage-earners who are working for the Government is furnished by taxation, and, as people cannot spend in other ways the money which the Government takes from them in taxes, the amount of money available for paying wages is not increased if there happens to be an addition to the number of Government workers, because there must be a corresponding fall in the demand for goods and services on the part of taxpayers. But in war-time all this is changed. It is taken for granted, though no one has attempted to prove it, that, as soon as war breaks out, nearly all the extra expenditure of a Government must be defrayed out of loans and not out of taxes. It follows from this assumption that when a Government begins to employ war-workers it pays their wages out of borrowed money. Here we get the first serious difference between peace-finance and war-finance. Large and increasing sums of money are paid out every week in wages to war-workers, but as this money is not obtained from taxpayers their pre-war demand for goods and services continues without serious restriction. At the same time, the new war-workers come into the market every week with their wages, and compete with the rest of the community. Consequently, prices rise.

There is a second economic consequence of war. As soon as hostilities commence Governments, as we have seen, require an enormous and increasing supply of goods and services; and, since the Governments must have what they require or lose the war, it follows that ordinary citizens cannot make their usual demand for food, clothing, travelling facilities, machinery, domestic labour, and so on, without impeding the efforts of their armies. In other words, they must not spend as much money as in peace-time. Obvious as it may appear now, this fact was not generally perceived or admitted in the early months of the war; at one time, indeed, the fashionable catchword was " business as usual." Had it been perceived, a most important inference could have been drawn, one which might have had a great and most useful influence on our war finance. This inference is that all citizens above the poverty line can bear a large addition to their taxation

as soon as war breaks out : we have seen that
they cannot spend as freely as they used to
spend, because of the' demands of the Army
and Navy, therefore they may just as well
hand over to the Chancellor of the Exchequer
the surplus which they cannot spend. In the
long run, he will take this surplus and a good
deal more ; if he takes it at once taxpayers
will be spared several unpleasant consequences, of which one is a more rapid growth
of the War Debt. Having thus explained
that the facts of the case demanded a large
addition to taxation as soon as the war broke
out, let us set in tabular form the state of the
national finances before the war and during
the first year of war. The actual receipts of
the last complete financial year before the
war, *i.e.* the twelve months ending March 31st,
1914, were as follows :

	£
Customs , ...	35,450,000
Excise	39,590,000
Estate Duties . . .	27,359,000
Income, Property, and Super Tax	47,249,000
Other Taxes . . .	13,381,000
Total Tax Revenue . .	163,029,000
Receipts from Non-Tax Revenue	35,213,897
Total Revenue . .	198,242,897

The Budget for 1914–15 provided for some small increases in revenue and expenditure, but before the second quarter was half through the war had begun. No immediate steps were taken to raise any further revenue, but there was so much alarm about the future, and at first so much difficulty in obtaining either credit or ready money, that prices did not rise ; in fact, the luxury trades and shops supplying men's clothing almost closed down for want of custom. This stage, however, did not last very long, although a glance at the *Economist's* index numbers will show that prices, except for food, actually fell during the first months of war.

Date.	Cereals and Meat.	Other Foods.	Textiles.	Minerals.	Miscellaneous.	Percentage change.
1901–5 average	500	300	500	400	500	100
End July, 1914	579	352	616½	464½	553	116·6
„ Aug. „	641	369	626	474	588	122·6
„ Sept. „	646	405	611½	472½	645	126·4
„ Oct. „	656½	400½	560	458	652	124·2
„ Nov. „	683	407½	512	473	684½	125·5
„ Dec. „	714	414½	509	476	686½	127·3

The change in prices shown above is exactly what one would expect, prices of food rise because people must have food, and the army is sure to consume more per head than the

civil population, partly because of waste,
partly because soldiers in training need extra
food ; but purchases of other things can wait,
so those prices fall. Under a sound system of
war finance something of this kind would
have continued all through the war : food
prices would have kept very high, prices of
clothing would have risen as suits and boots
wore out and had to be replaced ; but prices
of other things would have fallen, because
people would not have had money enough to
spend it on things which they could do without. And if taxation were adequate a further
influence working against high prices would
have been added.

The First War Budget

It was not until November 17th, 1914—
fifteen weeks after the outbreak of war—that
the Chancellor of the Exchequer brought in
his first War Budget. This was a very modest
measure, and was only accepted as a make-
shift or interim Budget. Mr. Lloyd George
simply doubled the Income Tax as it stood,
added threepence to the tea duty, and raised
the beer duty by an amount calculated to

increase the retail price by a halfpenny a
pint.

These additions to existing taxation were
assumed to be merely a rough-and-ready way
of raising a little more revenue, but every one
expected the regular Budget at the end of the
financial year would be a well-considered
measure, increasing all old taxes which
seemed to be open to additions and imposing
new taxes. Since no change had been made
in the graduation of the Income Tax all the
old anomalies were merely doubled. An
increase in the rate of the tax ought to have
been accompanied by an extension to a far
larger number of taxpayers : the limit of total
exemption, *e.g.* should have been lowered at
once to £100 a year.

As time went on the daily expenditure,
mainly out of borrowed money, grew steadily,
and the necessity for increased revenue
became more evident. But when April, the
usual Budget month, passed without a statement from the Chancellor of the Exchequer,
economists began to be alarmed, because any
Chancellor who is introducing fresh taxation
naturally wants to start at the earliest
moment in the financial year. On May 4th,

1915, Mr. Lloyd George rose to make his long-expected statement ; he prefaced it with a grave speech which pointed to heavy new taxes, and then, much to the surprise of the House of Commons, ran away from his own maxims and proposed no further taxation. Yet by this time expenditure had grown from his modest guess of £450,000,000 a year on November 17th to an estimate of £1,133,000,000 against which staggering total, as it then seemed, the estimated revenue was only about £272,000,000.

It may look as if I had given too much space to what is now ancient history ; unfortunately it was the Budget of the first ten months after August 4th, 1914, which determined how the war should be financed for the rest of its course and how the majority of citizens in this country should regard their own rights and duties in the matter. In these ten months the child was trained or the bough was bent in the way which it should grow. A small minority with fixed incomes perceived that they must economise, because their actual money income was slightly reduced by the doubled income tax, while they could foresee

that the tax must soon be increased. But the
vast majority, including practically all wage-
earners, only saw what was obvious and
pleasant, namely, that employment was good
and wages rising. They had more money to
spend than they had ever possessed before,
and they spent it freely, encouraged at one
time by the fashionable cry, "business as
usual."

In the first year of war the shortage of
commodities was not acute, we had the usual
large stock-in-trade and the check on imports
imposed by German submarines was not yet
serious. Consequently people could still spend
and consume freely. A few persons preached
economy, but Parliament gave no lead,
members being content to pocket their
salaries for doing very little work and to give
the Government a free hand. Before Mr.
Lloyd George left the Exchequer, therefore,
this habit of spending had become widespread,
and it seemed to be an accepted financial
principle that the war was to be paid for out
of loans, so long as taxation covered the
interest and a small redemption fund on
the borrowed money. No one could be
blamed for arguing "the Government spends

lavishly, Parliament is quite satisfied with the financial situation; why should I pretend to greater wisdom and deny myself the things which every one else is buying? "

CHAPTER II

THE RESULTS OF DELAY

IT is easy enough for a Government to postpone taxation, at any rate in the earlier months of a war, but it cannot postpone its expenditure. Millions of money have to be paid out every week as soon as the war begins, and later these millions are paid out every day. Since our Government lacked the courage to raise the money by taxation, for Mr. McKenna came to the Exchequer too late for an effective reversal of the financial policy adopted in the first ten months of the war, it has had to raise larger and larger War Loans.

Whether of necessity or not, it has paid higher rates of interest on each successive loan. We have already noticed that the money paid by the subscribers to War Loans comes from more than one source. Some people put their sovereigns in the Loan, other people borrow from their banker for the purpose ; large sums are subscribed by limited companies, and lastly, the banks put in subscriptions on their own account. Without going fully into the question, it may be said, broadly, that subscriptions out of savings have no effect on prices and that other kinds of subscriptions tend to force prices higher ; they cause what is known as "inflation."

The actual process is simple enough and can be explained without the use of technical terms. When a man saves £100 and buys a War Bond, or £100 worth of War Loan, he transfers to the Government a sum of money which he might have spent on buying things for himself and his family. With this money the Government buys shells and cartridges, *i.e.* pays the wages of the workpeople who make the shells, and they spend the money on much the same kind of things that the subscriber could have bought if he had not put it into War Loan. Consequently, the transaction has no influence on prices. But if our subscriber borrows £100 from his bank in order to buy War Loan, he increases the Government's spending power by £100 without reducing his own expenditure by one pound. Consequently, there is an extra £100 in the market buying food, clothes and what not, and so prices rise.

Before the war it was reckoned that the annual savings of people in the United Kingdom came to about £400 millions a year, this being one-sixth of the national income, which was estimated by the Treasury at £2,400 millions. These figures of course are estimates only, and not statistics, but there is nothing else to take their place. How far the saving habit has increased during the war it is impossible to tell. Rich people, no doubt, have cut down their personal expenditure enormously, but then the increased Income and Super Taxes have cut down their incomes too, unless they were shipowners or coal-owners or engaged in the war trades. Still they should have had large sums available for War Loans. A large number of new people have become rich owing to the war, and they have probably subscribed generously too ; but the professional classes, the small land-owners, and people with fixed incomes, whether *rentiers* or recipients of salaries, have had their money income cut down by Income Tax and their real income cut down still more by the rise in prices, so that they have little margin for saving. Quiet middle-class people who used to put by their hundred or two a year may have continued to do so, but instead of investing it they have had to pay over the money to the tax collector.

It seems probable therefore that a majority of the class who used to save before the war have not had much power of saving during the last four years. For any large sums we must go to the class which has had its income raised so remarkably as a direct result of the war, *i.e.* the owners of and workers in the war factories. The owners have had to contribute largely to the revenue through the Excess Profits Duty and the Munition Levy, but they must have had a good deal left over: the workers have been earning enormous wages, and, although they are at last liable to Income Tax, the tax collector will not take any large percentage owing to the abatement and allowances, unless their wages are over eight pounds a week. But as the rate of wages is immensely higher than they could have ex-pected to earn before the war, they have had a large margin out of which to save if they wished. Every kind of encouragement and

2

opportunity of saving and of investing in War Loans, War Bonds, or War Savings Certificates has been provided, and no doubt a large number have saved' considerable amounts. Unfortunately wage-earners in England, perhaps because we have no peasant proprietors, seldom have the saving habit ; it is to be feared that the good wages so easily earned have been as readily spent.

The conclusion to be drawn from such facts as we have is that the amount of money saved is quite small compared with the amount which the Government has borrowed. If that be so it seems to follow of necessity that a very large proportion of our War Loans have been obtained by " inflation." The Government gets its funds by an expansion of credit, there has been no corresponding production of commodities, consequently prices have been bound to rise. One need not hold the " Quantitative theory of money " in its strictest form in order to perceive the connection between prices and the amount of money in circulation. To take a simple illustration : let us suppose that we are at a seaside town, and go one morning to the market ; if the market is crowded with visitors who have obviously come to spend money we shall find that the prices of eggs, vegetables, flowers and so on are high. If on the other hand we go on a day rather out of the season, when the market is not filled with visitors but only with a few natives on the lookout for bargains, we shall find that the stallholders have put down their prices in order to attract the small sums of money which possible purchasers have brought to spend. In each case we have assumed that the quantity of eggs, vegetables and so on is the same. But suppose that one day in the season there is an unexpectedly large supply of eggs, etc., we shall see the price go down : if on another market-day the supply is smaller than usual, the price will rise. Prices, in short, are a relation between money and things. If there is plenty of money about prices will be high : if there are plenty of things to be bought and only the regular amount of money prices will be low.

What we have had during the past four years is a steadily increasing amount of money in the hands of the public and a steadily decreasing supply of goods for them to buy with it. These two economic forces working in the same direction are quite enough to account for the rise in prices. Some silly people talk about " profiteering," and denounce farmers and shopkeepers ; other silly people demand Government control of this, that, and the other thing, with prices fixed by some archangel in Whitehall. "Bring another bucket," they say, " and more mops, the place is getting flooded ! " Wouldn't it be simpler to turn off the taps ?

So long as the Government continues to pay for a war out of borrowed money prices must keep on rising. Food controllers may fix maximum prices as much as they like, the chief results of their efforts is to check production and so to make food scarce and therefore dearer than it would be if they left people to manage their own business. When prices began to rise in 1915 it was said " War always sends up prices." That is very largely true, but it ought not to send up all prices : under a sound financial system, *i.e.* one which paid for the war by taxes and not by loans, the prices of necessaries, such as food, clothing and coal, might rise, but the prices of luxuries and of non-necessaries would fall, because people would not have money enough to buy the latter. This was what actually happened in 1914: no one knew what was going to happen, so they bought nothing that they could do without. The true cause of the *universal* rise in prices is the Government's disbursement of borrowed money and its refusal to impose heavy direct taxation in the early months of war.

As prices rose higher and higher complaints became louder and louder, and the Government was called upon to bring them down. This was very much like calling upon Mrs. Pankhurst and her friends to form a fire brigade in order to deal with political incendiarism, and it was no less futile. The Government tried to bring down prices, it issued orders one day and reversed them the next; at different times it discouraged the keeping of cattle, pigs and poultry, or the making of cheese and milk. At one time it encouraged the farmer by guaranteeing him a minimum price and granting him exemption from the Excess Profits Duty; at another time it did its utmost to stop him making profits at all. In one thing only was it consistent, it refused to admit that a war demands sacrifices from the stay-at-home population and that its cost must be paid by the tax-payers.

How the taxpayers bear it, and whether the burden is fairly distributed among different classes of taxpayers must be discussed in a separate chapter.

CHAPTER III

WHEN the Chancellor of the Exchequer issues a War Loan for a thousand millions, what happens? Some people seem to think that the country is straightway £1,000 millions richer, because the citizens hold War Loan Stock to that amount. Other people are no less convinced that the country is poorer by just these amounts, because the Government has incurred a debt of £1,000 millions. Perhaps they are both equally wrong. Is not the real effect as follows? Holders of property and securities, including owners of War Loan, seem to be richer in the aggregate because they undoubtedly hold legal documents to the nominal value of £1,000 millions more than they had before the issue of the Loan, and their new security undoubtedly is a mortgage on or represents a share of the

23

national wealth to the extent of £1,000 millions.

But there is no more real wealth in the country than there was before ; the change which has taken place is just this—there are more mortgages on it, or there are more shares in it. The wealth is there just as it was before, only more people own it. The process is similar to the distribution of "bonus" shares by a limited company : the real capital is not increased, the market value is not increased, but it is split up among a greater number of shares, and the old shares are all less valuable in consequence. We now see what has happened as the result of the War Loans—all pre-existing securities have been lowered in value. This is not merely the scaling down of market prices in the Stock Exchange list which has followed the issue of Government stocks at $3\frac{3}{4}$, $4\frac{1}{2}$ and finally $5\frac{1}{4}$ per cent, serious as this loss of market value has proved. There is in addition a further loss, which is represented by the decline of the value of the pound sterling ; and the two combined have lowered the *real* value of pre-war gilt-edged securities by about one-half. Other kinds of property have not fallen in value to the same extent ; agricultural land has risen in *money* value, and perhaps in real value too, though the process is obscured by the reluctance of landlords to raise their rents. Houses have risen in money value, in fact the directors of the First Garden City, Ltd. have sent round a notice to their tenants at Letchworth asking them to have the insurance values of their houses raised. Shares in many industrial companies have risen in price, and naturally so, because the burden of paying interest on the debenture and preference stock has been lightened by the depreciation of the currency ; the case of shipping and coal-mining companies is too well known to require further mention.

We see, therefore, that the owners of certain kinds of property, such as Government and municipal loans, debentures and preference stock of every kind, or railway, gas, water, tramway and bank shares, have lost half what they possessed before the war. In making this calculation no allowance is added for the increase in Income Tax. The real financial burden of the war has fallen mainly on this class. Other kinds of property have fallen heavily in *real* value, though not in

" paper " value, *e.g.* mortgages, cottage property and some kinds of house property. The importance of these facts will be evident when we come to consider how the War Debt should be paid off.

The conclusion to which we are led is the rather startling one that the war has been paid for as it has gone on mainly by the owners of certain kinds of property. A further conclusion tells us that the fashionable plan of " making posterity pay " is impossible : we may leave many awkward problems for posterity to settle, but we cannot leave it to settle our war bill. It is curious how widely the idea of making posterity pay has prevailed ; nearly every one took it as an axiom that all war costs which were not met at the moment out of revenue must necessarily fall on posterity, and borrowing was justified on the ground that as the war was being waged in order to secure the safety of future generations those generations might fairly be asked to bear most of the cost. But recently economists who have tackled the question are being forced to admit that the war is paid for as it goes on, and that its cost cannot be thrown on posterity. Mr. Hartley Withers, in *Our Money and the State* (1917), explained that the war " has to be paid for now by somebody, and all wars have always been paid for during the time in which they were fought and finished up " (p. 30) ; " Our army cannot eat the bread that is going to be sown in 1930, or wear boots made out of hides whose original owners are yet unborn." Professor A. C. Pigou, in the *Economic Journal* of June, 1918 (page 137), appears to take the same view, so far at least as *internal* loans are concerned, for he writes : " In so far as a war is financed by loans contracted abroad, the present generation escapes the cost of it at the expense of future generations " : and ater, " Whatever internal debt posterityl will have to pay, posterity will also receive." Professor W. R. Scott comments on this sentence (*Economic Journal* for September, 1918, page 258) : " What posterity payr posterity will also receive—at the cost of earning it. Speaking quite generally, the effect of a loan is that posterity is rendered liable to do the amount of work which is necessary to pay it off." Dr. Scott appears to draw a distinction between the interest, which is no real burden, and the sinking fund, which is a burden.

Mr. Withers seems to have been the first person to state publicly that a war must be paid for as it goes on, but my own theory was in type, though not published, before Mr. Withers' book came out. That theory was outlined in an Appendix to the British Association (Economic Section) report for 1917: "This objection (to taxation) is founded on a mistaken belief, *i.e.* the belief that a nation can engage in a long war and yet evade the cost of it by throwing the burden on posterity."[1] The war, in short, has been carried on by sacrifices made *now*,[1] and all official juggling with prices, and money, and rations, and loans only serves to conceal the true facts from the nation ; it is possible, one must admit, that the official mind is just as blind to the facts as the public. Not only does the borrowing method conceal the facts, it leads directly to waste of money and waste of effort at a time when the country can least afford to waste anything. The " man in the street " knows little about economic laws, and is naturally inclined to

---

[1] *Industry and Finance* (1917) (Pitman and Son), p. 351.

believe that the Government will not adopt
the wrong policy in matters of finance merely
from want of courage. The Government tells
him that he can throw a large part of the cost
of the war on posterity, and has a right to do
so ; how can he find out for himself that
what the Government and its supporters in
the press tell him is untrue ?

CHAPTER IV

THE WAR BUDGETS

WE have seen how the floodgates of extravagance, public and private, were opened during the first ten months of war. As one looks back the amount spent seems small enough compared with our seven or eight millions a day now ; but it was the policy of spending freely then, which set the fashion and compels us to spend largely now.

However, the shortage in shells turned Mr. Lloyd George's energies in another direction, and all economists rejoiced when Mr. McKenna, who had made his reputation as Financial Secretary of the Treasury, came to the Exchequer. By the time that the new Chancellor had his plans ready for his first Budget (September 21st, 1915) our expenditure had grown to an estimated total of £1,590 millions a year. Thirteen and a half months had passed since the outbreak of hostilities before the nation was asked to face the financial facts of war, but at last it had a real War Budget. That the new Chancellor should bring in a Budget at all in September was an implied censure on his predecessor, such as would have made a Peel, or a Northcote, or a Gladstone retire from the Cabinet. The Budget of September 21st indeed did what should have been done as soon as the first financial disturbance caused by the war had settled down.

Mr. McKenna first took the Income Tax as Mr. Lloyd George had left it and raised it by 40 per cent, adding a new and heavier scale for the Super Tax. This was not the chief point. For some time past economists had recognised that the Income Tax, which began as a war tax, was only paid by a very small proportion of citizens. So long as the franchise was limited this was only fair ; so long as the tax itself was small the inequality was unimportant ; but when the tax had risen to 2s. 4d. in the pound and had become the sheet anchor of the Exchequer it was unjust and undesirable that a large majority of electors should escape direct responsibility

for the policy which their votes had endorsed
Since 1894 incomes below £160 a year had
been free from Income Tax, and in practice
wage-earners, even when getting £4 a week
and over, had escaped assessment : moreover,
the allowances in respect of children under
sixteen had raised the real exemption limit
well above the point fixed by Sir William
Harcourt.

Mr. McKenna boldly reduced the limit of
total exemption to £130 a year, lowered the
abatement from £160 to £120, and provided
that the wage-earner, if earning more than
fifty shillings a week, should be made to pay
his share. Then he added largely to indirect
taxation (sugar, tea, coffee, etc.) and to postal
and telegraph charges, and finally introduced
the most effective of war taxes—the Excess
Profits Duty. Naturally, as there was no
precedent for it, the estimate of the yield
from the new duty was a mere guess ; but
Mr. McKenna reckoned that his new taxes
would yield £107 millions in a full year, while
the probable revenue for the year ending
March 31st, 1916, was put at £305 millions.
That this was less than one-fifth of the
estimated expenditure was not Mr. McKenna's

fault, but it left £1,285 millions to be borrowed. The main items of this expenditure were as follows :

	Estimated £
Army	715,000,000
Navy	190,000,000
Advances to Allies . .	423,000,000
Pre- and Post-Moratorium Bills	36,000,000
Ordinary National Services, including Debt . . .	170,000,000
Food Supplies, etc. . .	56,000,000
Total	1,590,000,000

This proved a remarkably close guess, for the actual expenditure for one year turned out to be only £31 millions short : happily, too, the revenue forecast turned out to be under the mark.

Had this Budget been brought in earlier the whole course of our war finance would have been altered ; we should have escaped a considerable proportion of the War Debt, and we should have avoided part of the rise in prices with all the hardships and worries and discontents which high prices have brought upon us. When the Budget of May, 1915, added nothing to the Income Tax the propertied classes imagined that they were

3

escaping taxation ; as a matter of fact nothing could have been more disastrous for them than this seeming exemption—they saved a shilling then only to pay a pound later. At the time, however, things seemed to be going very well ; money was plentiful, thanks to Treasury notes and constant expenditure out of borrowed money, employment was good, wages, prices and profits rose steadily. The shortage of food and materials had hardly begun, and it looked as if the royal road to national prosperity was to engage in a big war. Hardly anyone troubled to look ahead and to ask what would happen if the war lasted another year, or even the three years said to have been foretold by Lord Kitchener.

The September measure was the real War Budget, for it fixed the main lines which our war finance has followed since then ; but Mr. McKenna's second Budget, introduced promptly at the beginning of the next financial year (April 4th, 1916), struck the popular imagination because it proposed to raise the revenue to the then unheard-of figure of £500 millions. It is not so many years since Mr. Gladstone thought that a hundred million Budget was the end of all things. Few changes of importance were made in the September scheme, but the Excess Profits Duty was raised from 50 to 60 per cent, and the yield from it, which had hardly begun to flow into the Exchequer before April, accounted for most of the estimated gain in the revenue. As a matter of fact the Treasury guess of £86 millions fell far short of the mark, for the new tax brought in almost £140 millions in 1916–17, and is now a more fruitful impost than the Income Tax itself. Nearly all the chief sources of revenue yielded more than the Budget estimate except Excise, which declined as a result of efforts to check the consumption of intoxicants, and Customs, which suffered from the restriction of imports. The chief items may be given as follows :

	Receipts. £	Estimate. £	+ or − £
Customs .	70,561,000	71,000,000	− 439,000
Excise . .	56,380,000	65,000,000	− 8,620,000
Income and Super Tax .	205,033,000	195,000,000	+ 10,033,000
Excess Profits Duty . .	139,920,000	86,000,000	+ 53,920,000
Post Office .	34,100,000	36,100,000	− 2,000,000
Stamps . .	7,878,000	7,000,000	+ 878,000
Miscellaneous	28,343,582	11,175,000	− 17,148,582
Total . .	573,427,582	502,275,000	+ 71,152,582

Unfortunately expenditure advanced in still greater proportions, being £2,198,113,000, or £372,733,000 above the original Budget estimate. The main items were as follows :

	£
Army, Navy, and Munitions	1,120,000,000
Miscellaneous . . .	30,000,000
Advances to Allies and Dominions . . .	450,000,000
Interest on Debt . .	138,500,000
Civil Service, etc. . .	60,000,000
Post Office . . .	27,000,000
Total	1,825,500,000

Up to this point we had two Budgets a year for the war period, and each time that a Chancellor faced a Committee of Wages and Means he had to admit a large increase of expenditure. And this increase, it must be remembered, was not a temporary one which would come to an end with the war ; some large items, such as the cost of guns and ammunition, or the food, pay and allowances of the troops, would cease, but pensions to widows or to the disabled, and the interest and sinking fund on the War Debt, would continue. After the Budget of April, 1916, the country had to wait a full year for its fifth

War Budget, and before Christmas the Coalition Ministry had resigned and Mr. Bonar Law had succeeded Mr. McKenna at the Exchequer

On May 2nd, 1917, Mr. Law introduced the fifth War Budget, and since this was four weeks later in the year than Mr. McKenna's last Budget it was assumed that his proposals, like those of Mr. Lloyd George's just two years earlier, would involve no important changes and no large additions to taxation. As a matter of fact, newspaper forecasts proved so accurate that Mr. Law felt it necessary to declare that there had been no leakage from the Treasury. Discarding the time-honoured rule that new taxation shall be kept a secret till the end of a Chancellor's exposition, he disclosed his plans early in his speech, saying, " I do not propose to add any new taxation whatever, and I only propose to make additions in the case of three existing taxes." These were the Excess Profits Duty, now raised from 60 to 80 per cent ; the Tobacco Duty, raised by 1s. 10d. in the pound, but subsequently lowered to 11d. ; and the Entertainments Tax, raised according to a scale which leaves penny and twopenny tickets unchanged. Next day he announced a fourth addition—an increase in the Dog Tax, *i.e.* a small addition for old dogs and a large one for new dogs. Both classes of dog, therefore, had their day; but for some undisclosed reason, possibly because there was so much life in the old dogs, their little license systems did not cease to be; it was the tax and not the dog that died. The proposal lingered for some time and was not finally dropped until July 19th. The three additions were expected to yield £27,500,000.

				£
Excess Profits	.	.	.	20,000,000
Tobacco	.	.	.	6,000,000
Entertainments	.	.	.	1,500,000

Why the Excess Profit Duty, which was estimated to yield £180 millions on the 60 per cent basis, should only yield £200 millions, or the 80 per cent basis, was not explained by Mr. Law. Many people have doubted the wisdom of raising the rate to so high a percentage : it is certain that in many cases the tax causes waste and extravagance, business men who have reached their pre-war standard are inclined to say, " The Government will pay four-fifths of anything

I spend now ; it is not worth while saving, and I may as well give a bonus to my staff." As it happened the Chancellor's estimate was largely exceeded, and the total yield of the Duty came to £220 millions.

This addition of £27½ millions to the taxation of thirteen months earlier was soon recognised to be wholly inadequate : such a sum is only just enough to cover the interest on £500 millions of War Loan or War Bonds, yet the Government continued to borrow at the rate of £500 millions every sixteen weeks. The *Economist* described the Budget as " a retrograde step in our financial policy " (May 5th), and referred four weeks later to " The Chancellor's paltry addition of six millions to permanent taxation in a Budget which shows a deficit of £1,650 millions." Colonel Godfrey Collins, M.P., who was soon to start a most valuable plan for increasing the financial powers of the House of Commons, summed up Mr. Law's proposals thus : " It is a permanent debt of £80 millions a year, and a permanent increase in taxation of £7½ millions a year." Neither the M.P. nor the *Economist* considered that the addition to the Excess Profits Duty was of any value for revenue purposes. But at last the House of Commons was awakening to its historic duties as guardian of the national purse. A memorial to the Chancellor of the Exchequer, signed by 187 members belonging to all parties, proposed :

"That a Committee be appointed, consisting of Members of this House, with power to review all national expenditure, examine Ministers and officials, and report to the House."

This was not a proposal to give the House any powers which it had not long possessed, but it was an assertion of its determination to use them, and the Government had to give way, only saving its face by stipulating that the Committee should not deal with questions of policy. The stipulation was obviously futile, for you cannot separate expenditure from policy, and the House of Commons is equally responsible for both. A strong Committee was appointed, and with Mr. Herbert Samuel as chairman, it set to work at once and soon began to publish reports on various departments which amazed the country by their revelations of official ineptitude.

The chief items of the 1917–18 Budget were as follows :

	Estimate. £	Actual Receipts. £
Customs	70,750,000	71,261,000
Excise	34,950,000	38,772,000
Estate Duties	29,000,000	31,674,000
Income and Super-tax	224,000,000	239,509,000
Excess Profits Duty	200,000,000	220,214,000
Stamps	8,000,000	8,300,000
Other Taxes	3,000,000	3,310,000
Total Tax Revenue	569,700,000	613,040,000
Post Office	33,700,000	35,300,000
Crown Lands, etc.	8,100,000	6,746,000
Miscellaneous	27,100,000	52,149,000
Total Revenue	638,600,000	707,235,000

Expenditure continued to increase and the estimate for the year came to £2,291,721,000, leaving £1,653 millions to be raised by loans. The chief items were :

	Estimate. £	Actual. £
Permanent Debt Charge	17,000,000	19,828,000
Interest on War Debt	194,500,000	170,023,000
Local Taxation Account, etc.	11,395,000	11,421,000
Supply Services	2,067,486,000	2,544,736,000
Total	2,290,381,000	2,697,000,000

The chief difference between the Budgets of 1917 and 1916 was that the Debt charge had grown by £80 millions ; the whole of this ought to have been met out of additional permanent taxation. As the year wore on sound views gathered strength, and when Mr. Bonar Law rose to expound his second Budget (April, 1918) every one was prepared for large additions to the existing taxes and for some novel taxes as well. At last the Chancellor showed a right sense of the duties belonging to his office and the requirements of war finance. Revenue had been coming in well all the year, and again the Excess Profits Duty brought in far more than the estimated sum ; but this time Mr. Law did not use the figures as an excuse for not increasing our taxes. There was, no doubt, another reason. The German offensive of March 21st had alarmed the country and military prospects had never looked darker, so the sacrifices asked from stay-at-home people seemed insignificant.

The principal change introduced by the 1918–19 Budget was an addition of a shilling to the Income Tax, the standard rate rising from the five shillings of Mr. McKenna's second Budget to six shillings. It is misleading, however, to talk of a five shilling or six shilling Income Tax, since only a small fraction of income tax payers actually pay that rate : companies are all charged at the standard rate and tax is deducted at that rate from all payments of "unearned." What individual taxpayers have to pay may be seen from the following tables, the first giving the 1916–17 and 1917–18 rates and the second the 1918–19 rate. In the case of parents (and now also of married men under varying income limits) there are further allowances, which raise the limits of total exemption, in the case of a man with a wife and three children (under sixteen years old) to £120 + 25 + 75, *i.e.* to £220 a year. It will be seen that Mr. Law did not alter the rate for incomes under £500 a year, and as he was the first to give the allowance of the tax on £25 in respect of a wife, he actually *lowered* the Income Tax for married men with less than £500 a year.

	Mr. McKenna, 1916.					Mr. Law, 1918.			
Income.	*Earned.*		*Unearned.*			*Earned.*		*Unearned.*	
£	*s.*	*d.*	*s.*	*d.*		*s.*	*d.*	*s.*	*d.*
130 to 500 .	2	3	3	0	...	2	3	3	0
500 to 1,000 .	2	6	3	6	...	3	0	3	9
1,000 to 1,500 .	3	0	4	0	...	3	9	4	6
1,500 to 2,000 .	3	8	4	6	...	4	6	5	3
2,000 to 2,500 .	4	4	5	0	...	5	3	6	0
Above 2,500 .	5	0	5	0	...	6	0	6	0

Again we perceive the fault of the First War Budget repeated, and indeed made worse. When the general rates of the tax are increased the limit of total exemption should be lowered at the same time, in order that the pecuniary sacrifice of all citizens shall be as nearly as possible equalised according to their means. Moreover, the occasion was exceptionally favourable, because Mr. Law was proposing to give an allowance for the first time to married men ; it would have been so easy and so evidently fair to say : " I will give an allowance of the tax on £30 to all married men, but I must lower the abatement and exemption limit to £100."

The Super Tax was increased very heavily, so much so that the combined effect of the two taxes is to take more than half his income from a man with £43,000 a year.

CHAPTER V

GROWTH OF THE WAR DEBT

OUR review of the six War Budgets shows a steadily expanding tax revenue, but at the same time a much larger growth of debt. During the ninety-eight years after Waterloo the country had prided itself on the consistency with which it set aside something out of revenue each year in order to lessen that legacy of the Napoleonic Wars—the National Debt. Only in twelve of those years did an addition take the place of a reduction, and by March 31st, 1914, the £900 millions of 1816 had been reduced to £651 millions.

Fortunately our Government cannot, in the ordinary way, spend money without the sanction of the House of Commons; so its first act on the outbreak of war is to obtain a Vote of Credit. These Votes continue at ir-regular intervals during the war, and, like

other war requirements, grow larger : only
£362 millions were needed in the first eight
months of the war, but the year 1915–16
needed £1,420 millions and 1916–17 took
£2,010 millions. When the Government has
obtained its Votes of Credit, it can raise and
spend the money as it likes, the only practical
check being the necessity of coming to the
House. again when more money is wanted.
Members of Parliament showed the greatest
readiness to vote whatever the Government
demanded—even the unprecedented sum of
£650 millions, on July 20th, 1917.

The Government borrows money for war
purposes in several ways, of which the most
obvious is a huge War Loan widely adver-
tised. The first big Loan was issued on
November 17th, 1914, the rate of interest
being 3½ per cent and the price £95, redeem-
able at £100 between 1925 and 1928, so that
the real rate was between 3¾ and 4 per cent.
Only £332 millions were raised by this Loan,
and soon after Mr. McKenna came to the
Exchequer he found it necessary to appeal
for a very much larger sum. The second War
Loan (June 21st, 1915) offered the flat rate of
4½ per cent, being issued at £100, and since

the 3½ Loan had fallen below its issue price
the Chancellor encouraged subscriptions to
his new Loan by offering to take the old Loan
in part payment for the new, anyone who
held £100 of the 3½ per cent being allowed to
exchange into 4½ per cents by subscribing a
further £105, thus getting £200 of the new
stock.   With the same idea of reassuring
investors, Mr. McKenna undertook that in
the event of a further *long period* Loan holders
should have the right of converting their
4½ per cent stock into it at par.

The attractive terms of the new Loan had
a devastating effect on Stock Exchange
Securities : the chief railway stocks fell four
or five points during the week, Canadian
Pacifics fell from £161 to £152, and the
aggregate depreciation was enormous.   This
fact suggests two reflections (1) that the issue
of a big Loan at an attractive price causes a
general fall in the value of pre-existing
securities, (2) that " attractive terms " may
not be necessary, and (3) that the subscribing
classes would really be better off if there were
some kind of a compulsion to take up a proportion of each new Loan at a rate not above
the previous market value.   It is part of my

theory of War Finance that each successive
Loan involves as much sacrifice on the part
of the propertied classes as they would have
to make under a large addition to direct
taxation.

In the case of the first two War Loans a
considerable proportion of the money subscribed was merely borrowed from the banks,
thus causing " inflation." If a man saves £100
and lends it to the Government, the latter
can only spend what the man did not spend,
and so prices are not raised (apart from the
natural tendency of Governments to spend
lavishly) ; but if he borrows the £100 from his
banker the Government has an extra £100
to spend, and there are £200 competing for
100 pounds' worth of goods, and so prices
rise.

It is doubtful whether so high a yield need
have been offered ; the *Economist's* Stock
Exchange correspondent wrote (June 26th) :
" The mere look of a 4½ per cent British
Government stock at par is held to be sufficient to upset most preconceived ideas of
investment " ; probably a 4 per cent issue at
£98 would have gone just as well. Many
patriotic people, in their desire to subscribe

for the Loan, sold older investments, such as railway stocks, and as the price of these was scaled down to the new level established by the 4½ per cent issue they had actually less money to lend than they would have had for a 4 per cent issue.

A big Loan causes much dislocation in the money market, requires a vast amount of advertising to make it a success, and involves an indefinite amount of inflation, consequently an alternative seemed to be wanted. This alternative is well described by its inventor, Mr. Drummond Fraser, of Manchester, as " continuous day by day borrowing " ; and the results of his proposal, explained in the reports of the Economic Section of the British Association for 1915 and 1916,[1] are now universally known as National War Bonds.[1] They have become, in fact, the main source on which the Chancellor of the Exchequer depends for his long-term borrowing. They are so successful that they may be regarded as the chief financial discovery of the war.

Treasury Bills and Exchequer Bonds are the means by which a Chancellor raises money

[1] (1.) *Credit Industry and the War*, 1915 (Pitman and Son), p. 251, and (2) *Labour Finance and the War*, 1916, p. 321.

4

for short periods—three, six, nine, or twelve
months. The rates of interest paid for these
short-term loans obey the same law as other
forms of borrowing, they rise gradually : the
rate for three month bills was 2¾ on April 14th,
1915, on August 9th it was 4½, on October 27th
4¾, and on November 12th it rose to 5 per cent.

Opinion in the City of London gets nervous
when the amount of Treasury Bills outstanding rises above £1,000 million. So on
January 11th, 1917, Mr. Bonar Law announced
the terms of the Third War Loan ; and this
time the rate of interest offered was no less
than 5¼ per cent, the Loan being a 5 per cent
stock issued at £95. All the arrangements in
connection with the issue were extremely
well-managed and the Loan proved an immense success. Simultaneously a 4 per cent
income-tax-compounded Loan was offered at
£100, but the applications were surprisingly
meagre, only some £22 million being applied
for ; yet it was clearly a more desirable investment for companies and for individuals with
incomes above £2,000 a year, since the Income
Tax was almost certain to be raised. A
British Government Loan yielding 5¼ per cent
would have seemed incredible a few years ago,

or even in 1915 ; and as has been said already, the rate of interest offered in our War Loans is probably excessive. Yet Mr. Law stated that he had been advised to offer 6 per cent ! Somewhat rashly he declared that no future Loan would offer any higher rate of interest ; this declaration was intended, no doubt, to hurry up the subscription of persons who might otherwise have waited for a 5½ per cent Loan. In order to maintain the market price of the 5 or 4 per cent Loans Mr. Law introduced a new piece of financial machinery which has been severely criticised ; this was a " Depreciation Fund," by which the Treasury undertook to set aside monthly a sum equal to one-eighth of 1 per cent of the amount of each Loan to form a fund to purchase stocks of either Loan for cancellation whenever the market price falls below the issue price. Financial purists declared that a true Sinking Fund could only be formed when the revenue exceeded the expenditure : that is true, but this is not called a Sinking Fund, although for the purpose of the third War Loan it would have acted as a Sinking Fund but for the option of converting their bonds into the Loan given to holders of National

War Bonds.   Still it is an expensive bit of
machinery, for the taxpayer, in effect, is
borrowing in order to pay off debt, and so
loses a turn in each transaction.

WAR BORROWING

It seems to be taken for granted that a
Government must borrow the greater proportion of the money which it requires for a war.
This theory however has not always been
accepted, nor is it universally held even now,
and the holders have seldom troubled to work
out their theory, still less to demonstrate its
applicability to the present war.   The varied
views of different schools of war-financiers
are discussed with much learning by Professor
W. R. Scott, in his " Jevons Memorial Lecture
for 1918 "[1] (pp. 43–64).   The earlier, which he
calls the British theory, was that " all war
expenditure should be obtained from taxes
levied while the war was in progress : to this
was opposed the German theory, that all war
expenditure ought to be met by loans."   It is
a curious fact that the " all tax " theory was

[1] *Economic Problems of Peace after War.*   Cambridge
University Press.

held by Adam Smith, Ricardo, Chalmers, M'Cullock and J. S. Mill at a time when our tax system was far less developed than it is now, When a Government relies for its revenue on indirect taxes, even if supplemented by a property tax, the limits are soon reached beyond which an increase of the tax on any given commodity is followed by such a fall in the consumption of that commodity that the yield from the tax begins to fall too. But with an Income Tax so highly developed and so effective as our own the possibilities of taxation are indefinitely extended : indeed there is just all the difference in the world between our system, which depends on direct taxation supplemented by a few taxes on widely-used " luxuries," and the continental systems, which depend mainly on indirect taxes. The German financial edifice crumbled as soon as war broke out, and the Government was afraid to publish the actual figures of revenue ; her three Allies were in a still worse state.

CHAPTER VI

LOANS OR TAXES

THE controversy between borrowers and taxers has so important a bearing on our subject it must be treated at some length. It is customary to say that a Government which goes to war must spend such huge sums of money that no endurable plan of taxation could provide them. This is perfectly true if reliance is placed upon indirect taxation ; how far it is true when the taxation is mainly direct remains to be discussed. Elsewhere,[1] in an appendix to the British Association report, I have admitted that there are payments which a Government may fairly make out of borrowed money, *e.g.* for land, buildings, ships, and other things of permanent value, partly because these things are of the nature of capital, partly because the sellers are not likely to treat the

---

[1] *Industry and Finance* (1917), pp. 350, 351.

purchase money as income. Secondly there are the supplies, munitions, and so on, purchased *abroad* : these may also be purchased with borrowed money, because the money, or something in its place, goes out of the country. In the case of a small war, with only one or, perhaps, two countries on each side, much of the military material required by both sides can and probably will be obtained from neutrals : perhaps the neutrals will give credit, perhaps they will insist on payment in some form ; in either case the belligerent will not feel bound to pay the bill out of tax revenue. But in a world-war like the present one there are hardly any neutrals, what each belligerent needs he has to produce for himself or beg from his Allies. In the United Kingdom we produce most of the things which our own armies and fleets require, and a good deal for our Allies as well. The real question therefore is " How should the things which the Government buys in the United Kingdom be paid for ? "

It is my contention that they should be paid out of revenue and not out of borrowed money. Let us see what really happens. Every week the War Office requires so many shells, cartridges, guns, rifles, waggons, carcases of meat, sacks of flour, tunics, trousers, puttees, boots, and a thousand and one other things. All these (apart from any supplies we may get from North and South America) are being made every week in this country, and the makers get paid for making them every week. Yet the wages of the war-workers are paid out of borrowed money! There is no more reason for paying the wages of Government employees out of borrowed money in war-time than there is in peace-time. That the number of such employees is much larger has no relevance, because the number of wage-earners employed on private work must be proportionately less, and the money which would normally have gone to pay the peace-worker should be diverted by the Chancellor of the Exchequer to pay the war-workers. Such a diversion would involve no greater hardship on the rest of the community than is inseparable from a great war. People of all classes ought to have seen as soon as war broke out that they must do without some of the things and conveniences to which they were accustomed : if they were wealthy they had more scope for a patriotic self-sacrifice, but whatever their station they ought to have recognised that they could not maintain their pre-war standard of living.

The duty of making this clear belonged pre-eminently to Parliament and to the Cabinet, and the individual who should have been the spokesman for both was the Chancellor of the Exchequer. He should have made it plain to every one that the motto should be not "Business as usual," but " Nothing as usual, and sacrifice for every one." The simplest and most effective method of imposing this truth on every one was to increase taxation : as soon as war on the European scale began it was inevitable that taxation on a correspondingly vast scale must follow, the only effect of postponing taxation was to make it much heavier in the end, just as the only effect of postponing repairs is to make them much more costly when they are finally effected ; indeed the analogy is rather with the omission to stop a leak, because there is not only the larger repair to be done later, but the incalculable damage and loss through the escape of water.

It may be argued also that a larger addition to our taxes would have involved very little more immediate sacrifice than was the inevitable result of a state of war. The economic difference made by war is that people in general cannot buy the same things or as many things as they used to buy because the things are not there. In peace-time people cannot buy all that they want because they haven't money enough ; in war-time their purchases are curtailed, whether they have much money or little, because there is a smaller stock of goods to be bought. The real sacrifice made by the non-combatant in war-time is his abstention from consuming the things which he was accustomed to have. If his extra taxation just takes away that proportion of his income which he cannot spend (because the things he would have bought are not available) he makes very little more real sacrifice than he is bound to make, whatever the Chancellor of the Exchequer may do. This is only one of the reasons why a Finance Minister should add largely to direct taxation as soon as war breaks out.

There are other weighty considerations which point to the same policy. Some weeks, perhaps, must escape before the economic side of war gets the attention which it deserves ; troops have to be mobilised and despatched, coasts to be guarded, recruiting to be started and services of all kinds to be improvised. But as early as October, 1914, it had become evident that the Government would need to command the services of an immense number of new employees, mainly for the making of guns, rifles, shells and ammunition, but also for the supply of other warlike material. It ought to have been equally evident that this army of war-workers could not easily be recruited if the rest of the community continued its usual peace-time demand for goods and services ; consequently the rest of us could not spend what we had been accustomed to spend in buying things for ourselves without depriving our fighting forces of indispensable supplies of munitions, material and food ; a further logical deduction ought to have been drawn—all non-fighting citizens who had incomes above the poverty line ought to pay heavy, immediate and direct taxation.

If the Chancellor of the Exchequer, towards the end of 1914, had seen things as they really were, he would have realised that the right policy was to enforce economy by adding largely to taxation. By so doing he would have reduced the public demand for commodities at a time when the supply of commodities was quite certain to be smaller. Thereby he would have checked, even if he failed to prevent entirely, the rise in prices which was otherwise inevitable, and he would have lowered the taxpayer's War Bill, since the Government is the chief buyer of commodities in war-time. Further, as a consequence of the increased revenue and decreased expenditure thus secured, he would have avoided a large part of the enormous War Loans which have shaken British credit so severely. During the South African War Sir M. Hicks Beach could borrow at 2¾ per cent, now Mr. Bonar Law has to offer 5¼ per cent.

" But," it may be objected, " the taxpayer would not endure the sacrifice involved in heavy taxation, say a five-shilling income tax at the beginning of the war." Undoubtedly he would dislike the idea very much, although it is a trifle compared with the sacrifice exacted from our soldiers ; but if the taxpayer imagines that he can have a big war without paying for it he is woefully mistaken, and the sooner he learns the truth the better. He will be hardly less mistaken if he thinks that he can have the war now and pay for it later, or possibly throw the cost on "posterity," although nearly every one believes that posterity will pay most of the cost.

As a matter of fact a nation has to pay for its wars as they go on, unless it can borrow from other nations. Mr. Hartley Withers has pointed out that you cannote at bread made from next year's wheat, or wear clothes from the wool of sheep as yet unshorn. Nor is it possible to avoid present sacrifices by postponing taxation. An income is only worth what it will buy, and already the rise in prices has taken at least one-third out of the purchasing power of the pound sterling. This has the same effect as an Income Tax of 6s. 8d. in the £1 on *all* incomes, and it is a much heavier burden than any conceivable Income Tax because it takes as large a percentage from the poor man as from the millionaire. Therefore the sacrifice has been made, although the taxpayer has not been credited with his payment. Indeed the case is much worse than that ; his War Bill has gone on as if he were making no sacrifice at all, and the 6s. 8d. in the £1 has been added to the Bill. Ever since the war began the Chancellor of the Exchequer has been putting up prices against himself. If he had imposed heavy taxation at the outset he would have lowered the purchasing power of individual Englishmen, but he would have kept up the value of the English sovereign, and consequently the money cost of the war would have been much lower.

One incidental advantage of taxation at the outset is that it gives the Government greater power over economic condition. If people had been forced to pay heavy taxes in 1914–15 they would either have spent less, thereby reducing the demand for such things as food, clothing, coal, steel, shipping and transport, which were needed more and more for our fighting forces, or they would have worked harder in order to make up their incomes, thus increasing the supply of commodities— a highly desirable result. But it would not be the only good result. When war breaks out hundreds of thousands of citizens, both men and women, must change their occupations entirely in order that the munitions and other supplies required by the Army may be provided. Drastic taxation, by diverting the ordinary demand of the public for things which can be done without, would have set free persons engaged in the non-essential trades, who would have found a ready market for their services in munition and other war factories.

If the taxation had been heavy enough it would have had another advantage. It would have induced people who were doing no work at all to look round for some means of earning money, and so would have forced them to do something useful, and people who were doing unproductive work would have been forced into productive occupations. No doubt the change would have been unpleasant for them, but compared with life in the trenches this would have been the mildest of hardships. In any case the war taxation would have made people more ready to work in the war industries, and the enormous wages which the Minister of Munitions thought it necessary to offer, in order to attract workers into his factories, would not have been required. Again, we may see how the money cost of the war would have been reduced if taxation had been raised to a high pitch in the early days of the war instead of being postponed until the habit of lavish spending had become fixed.

CHAPTER VII

THE PEACE BURDEN

IT is still too early to say with certainty how large the War Debt will be when demobilisation is complete, or has advanced so far that the Government can stop borrowing. But we may reckon on a total debt of not less than £8,000 millions. This is not wholly due to the present war, for we started the war with a National Debt of £710 millions. More than half of this has been "converted" into War Loan, and in the process part of the capital was wiped out, although the rate of interest on the new stock was raised. There are, too, numerous assets which must be set against the huge total of debt; of these the chief are the loans made to our Allies and Dominions. These loans were stated by the Chancellor of the Exchequer, on November 12th, 1918, to have amounted to £1,683,500,000 on October 19th, the small proportion of £218½ millions being the amount advanced to our Dominions. During the rest of the financial year 1918–19 the loans to Allies and Dominions were expected to increase to something like £1,860 millions. Mr. Law's statement on November 12th was exceedingly confused.

Since the Debt grows by a million every few hours it is necessary to take some given date for our calculation. On November 30th, 1918, the net amount borrowed for the war was £6,501 millions. The total liabilities came to £7,213½ millions.

In round figures we may reckon on a total Debt of some £8,000 millions on April 1st, 1919. Against this we may set so much of the amounts lent to our Allies as we may think " good debts," but it seems inconceivable that we should attempt to recover money lent to Serbia or Belgium, and the amount lent to Russia may as well be written off at once as a bad debt. Mr. Bonar Law is fond of reckoning various other items against the Debt, such as the supplies of food, etc., in hand, but it seems doubtful whether these will turn out to be realisable in cash. Perhaps we may reckon on £200 millions from the

Dominions, £500 millions from our Allies, and say £50 millions from other sources. But these are only " good debts " and not cash, whether we shall obtain interest at first on the capital remains to be seen : it may very likely prove that those expenses of demobilisation which will be defrayed out of borrowed money will exceed the ultimate value of our " good " book debts.

It will be safer, therefore, to reckon on a Debt of £8,000 millions by the time that our financial system has got back to the only sound condition—i.e. all expenditure defrayed out of revenue. A Chancellor of the Exchequer at some future date—say April, 1920—will have to present a Budget somewhat as follows :

	£
Interest on War Debt (5 %) .	400,000,000
Sinking Fund „ (½ %) .	40,000,000
Pensions	60,000,000
General Expenditure . .	250,000,000
Total	750,000,000

At first sight there is nothing in this total which appears beyond the productivity of taxation as we have it now, for the estimated revenue in the Budget for 1918–19 was

£842 millions, which leaves an apparent
surplus of £92 millions. But the largest item
in that estimate was the £300 millions from
the Excess Profits Duty, and as that Duty
was *ex hypothesi* a tax on extra profits due to
the war, it can hardly be continued when the
war itself is over, and without it there will be
a deficit, not indeed of £200 millions, for the
abolition of the Duty should increase the yield
of the Income Tax, while the removal of in-
numerable restrictions should increase the
yield of Customs and Excise, but of something like £150 millions. This seems so
enormous a sum to raise out of Income Tax,
even when assisted by Customs and Excise,
that some people give up the idea in despair.
They declare that it is impossible to meet the
interest on £8,000 millions out of tax revenues,
therefore the War Debt, or a large part of it,
must be extinguished by one heroic operation ;
this operation they call a " Capital Levy,"
or the " Conscription of Wealth." The
proposal is so novel, and has such serious
consequences, that it requires at least a
chapter to itself.

CHAPTER VIII

THE CAPITAL LEVY

THE demand for a Capital Levy is supported by three main arguments, of which the first is the supposed impossibility of raising by taxation the four hundred millions or so a year which are required to pay the interest on the War Debt. This argument, which is not much more than a statement of opinion, may be left for future consideration. The second and more serious argument is that as young men have been compelled to sacrifice their lives in the war, stay-at-home people shall be compelled to sacrifice part of their property. As thus stated the theory has much plausibility. It is only the particular application of the theory to which objection can be taken. One aim, indeed, of this book is to shew that this principle ought to have been put into operation at the outbreak of the war. If it had been, we should not have heard anything about a Capital Levy. Undoubtedly when the war broke out the Government and the House of Commons, as the persons responsible for bringing Great Britain into the war, should have explained beyond all possibility of misunderstanding that to take part in such a war meant sacrifices, and heavy sacrifice too, on the part of every one in our country. For some persons, *i.e.* our soldiers and sailors, the sacrifices must be infinitely greater than those of the majority who stay safely at home, but that fact merely makes it an obligation of honour for the rest of us to do what we can. Every one who is left at home and does not absolutely starve to death is better off than the men in the trenches. We ought to have adopted the principle that no one should be better off financially than the fighting men and their families : in some cases the principle was in fact adopted, *e.g.* by the tribunals under the Compulsory Service Act, who have insisted that men exempted from military service shall undertake specified work for a labourer's wage. Thus one wealthy man, who was exempted in this way by a tribunal, undertook to work as an agricultural labourer at 25s. a week, and other men have had to give up their former occupations—*e.g.* teaching—and do manual work. No one suggests that these men have any grievance, people are much more inclined to say " How lucky they are to escape the discomforts, the cold, heat, hunger, fatigue, and the risk of wounds and death, which are inseparable from the soldier's life ! " Quite true, they *are* lucky, and so are all the rest of us.

We who stay at home while others fight for us ought at least to be willing to pay them their shilling or eighteen-pence a day and the allowance for their wives and children. No less clearly ought we to pay the wages of those who are working in war factories to supply our soldiers with shells, ammunition and other military necessities. In fact all the daily and weekly payments made by the Admiralty, the War Office, or the Ministry of Munitions should be provided directly by the taxpayers. This implies an Income Tax with a very much lower exemption limit, and the amount of income which should be entirely exempt from taxation seems to be plainly decided for us by the pay and allow-

ances of the private soldier. This principle
once settled that "Those who don't fight must
pay," the rest is a mere matter of arithmetic
—so much wanted by the Chancellor of the
Exchequer, so much to be raised by Income
Tax. Many other things would be simplified
too, we should probably not need an Excess
Profits Duty, as there would be no excessive
profits to tax, and there would be no case for
war bonuses in addition to wages, partly
because the soldier does not get them and
partly because prices would not be inflated,
as they have been by the spending of borrowed money. Rationing of the more important articles of general consumption, such
as milk, meat, and coal might be necessary,
but mere waste and extravagance would be
sufficiently checked by taxation.

If, then, anyone talks about the "Conscription of Income" he must be welcomed
as a patriot ; but the Conscription of Capital
is an entirely different matter. The first
means a general sharing of war burdens,
which makes for efficiency and concentra-
tion of national effort on the war ; the
second means the shifting of the financial
burdens on to the shoulders of a limited

class, and not even the class with the largest aggregate income. A remarkable Inland Revenue return comes out as I write this paragraph, which shows that the number of persons assessed as having incomes over £3,000 a year, *i.e.* Super-Taxpayers, actually fell from 30,211 in 1914–15 to 28,473 in 1915–16—the first war year—while the aggregate incomes showed a corresponding decline from £244¾ millions to £225 millions. For the second war year, 1916–17, the number of assessments increased to 29,723, *i.e.* nearly to the pre-war total, and the aggregate income came to three millions more (£247¼ millions). The meaning of this Super-Tax return will be discussed a few pages further on, for the moment I need only say that it shows how small a proportion of the national income is taken by the class who pays the highest rates of taxation. It may be admitted, however, that the second argument is a sound one so far as it attacks the financial system adopted at the beginning of the war; it proves the case for a higher Income Tax while the war lasts, but not the case for a Capital Levy when the war is over.

The third argument for a Capital Levy is
the one which appears to have secured most
support for the proposed confiscation. It
asserts that the propertied classes " have
made money out of the war " and consequently that they ought to bear the money
cost of it. This argument has been maintained widely in the Press and on the plat-
form of the Liberal and Socialist parties, it
has secured support in certain Liberal organs,
and every now and then the supposed fact
has been asserted in organs of a different
political complexion, such as the *Daily Mail*
and the *Daily Express*, which have a special
claim to voice the opinion of the man in the
street on economic questions.

Usually this argument takes the vague
form of a denunciation of " profiteering,"
one class after another being accused of
making excessive profits out of the war
because they charge the market price for
their goods. But sometimes we get the
statement in a definite form : thus, in the
Daily News of September 8th, 1917, Mr. A. G.
Gardiner declared that " the capital of the
individuals of the nation has increased during
the war from £16 thousand millions to £20

thousand millions." The *Nation* of October 6th, 1917, adopted Mr. Gardiner's figures, but inserted an important qualification—"the capital value of private property in the country, as expressed in money." These last four words are extremely important, they really destroy the whole argument based on the supposed increase of capital, for the increase is only alleged to be one quarter, while the fall in the purchasing power of money, even in October, 1917, was at least one third. In another issue the *Nation* asserted that "numbers of business men and investors should be making large sums of money out of the war," and again, "the possessing classes will have gained in the monetary value of their property by the war." In fact the estimates of the *Daily News* and the *Nation*, when tested by the purchasing power of our inflated paper money, tend to prove what one would expect to find, *i.e.* that the real capital of the country has been diminished by the war. If the scrip of the £6,000 or £7,000 millions of War Debt held internally is to be counted as capital, one might admit that the "capital expressed in money" has increased during the war. In fact it is only capital so far as it is represented by things of permanent value, such as manufactories, machinery, buildings and railways, to the extent of their post-war value, probably an insignificant proportion of the total. The War Debt resembles the mortgages of the spendthrift or the litigant, rather than those of the landowner who has borrowed in order to convert wastes or marshes into plough lands and meadows. Except for the post-war value of the war factories and of any plant brought back from abroad, which will be relatively small, all the War Debt represents money which has been spent unproductively, and money so spent cannot increase the national wealth.

Support for the view that war increases the national wealth comes from unexpected quarters; Professor A. C. Pigou, in the *Economic Journal* for April, 1918 (page 153), says :—" I hazard the guess that apart from the New War Loan Securities the value of the country's capital will be much the same after the war as in 1916–17. This means that, counting the new War Loan, it will come to somewhere about £16,000 millions, or half as much again as it was immediately before the war." It is an obvious deduction from this statement that a country which wants to get rich quickly should start a big war and then borrow enormous sums, since the longer the war lasts and the more money is borrowed the richer the country will become; and our view that Germany and Austria have been ruined by the war and their borrowings must be entirely reversed. Mr. Pethick Lawrence, in his recent book, *A Levy on Capital*,[1] says (page 43), "The well-to-do classes will not merely possess, as they did before, the greater part of the existing wealth of the country, they will also through their holdings in War Loan have a lien upon an immense part of the wealth produced in the future"; and again (page 44), "The distribution of wealth will be still more unequal when the war ceases than it was when it began, for the small number of rich men will retain most of what they had before and in addition they will have added the right to participate, because of their holdings in War Loan (bought largely out of profits on war contracts) in a great part of

[1] G. Allen and Unwin, Ltd. 2s. 6d. net.

the wealth which future generations will create."

Let us see what foundation there is for these views, which run so directly counter to the older opinion that war is a process which destroys wealth instead of creating it. It is singularly fortunate that the Super-Tax return should have been published at this moment (October 21st, 1918), since it gives the exact figures, not otherwise procurable, of the changes in income among the wealthier classes since the war. Had it been available when Professor Pigou and Mr. Lawrence wrote they would have perceived that their hypothesis of a large addition to the pre-war wealth of the well-to-do or of the propertied classes was not borne out by the investigations of Somerset House. "Where," the *Westminster Gazette* asks in surprise, " are all the people who were believed to be making great fortunes out of the war ? They do not make their influence felt in this return " (October 21st). It cannot be argued that the year in the return (1916–17), does not cover a period during which war profits were being made : it actually covers the period of the highest shipping profits and of the lowest series of the Excess Profits Duty, while all the Blue-book rates and most of the price-fixing and other methods for reducing profits came later.

The Super-Tax return is even more remarkable than it appears at first sight, and must be dealt with at some length. As reported in the newspapers of October 1st, 1918, no notice was taken of the fact that the figures for 1914–15 were described in the Inland Revenue Commissioners' report [1] as "final figures," while those for the next two years were both marked "Assessments made at 30th April, 1918." They are all shown in the two tables on pages 80–81.

A paragraph at the head of the page giving the return explains that the figures for any period are not finally settled for about three years : " the Special Commissioners continue to receive returns for the years 1915–16, 1916–17 and 1917–18, and complete statistics for those years are not available. The latest information indicates that the total income ultimately to be dealt with, the yield of the tax, and the number of persons chargeable

[1] Cd. 9151.

Class		Year 1914-15 (final figures).		Year 1915-16 (Assessments made at 30th April, 1918).	
Exceeding £	Not exceeding £	Total Incomes Assessed.[1] £	Number of Persons.	Total Incomes Assessed.[1] £	Number of Persons.
3,000	5,000	59,776,245	15,524	55,958,560	14,613
5,000	10,000	63,986,138	9,404	62,351,218	9,148
10,000	15,000	30,781,522	2,561	28,289,647	2,327
15,000	20,000	17,825,202	1,034	15,704,532	910
20,000	25,000	11,933,289	537	10,671,917	478
25,000	35,000	14,531,150	495	12,614,281	434
35,000	45,000	9,089,312	229	8,102,215	203
45,000	50,000	3,965,927	85	3,244,430	68
50,000	55,000	3,240,816	61	2,258,990	43
55,000	65,000	4,497,785	75	4,047,129	68
65,000	75,000	3,306,268	47	2,973,556	43
75,000	100,000	5,988,198	69	4,861,222	56
100,000		15,848,181	90	14,755,981	82
Total		244,769,134	30,211	225,833,678	28,473

[1] Adjustments made under Section 6 of the Finance Act, 1912 (which provides for the collection of a proportionate part only of the year's super-tax in the case of a person dying during the year of charge) have not been taken into account

Class.		Year 1916–17 (Assessments made at 30th April, 1918).	
		Total Incomes Assessed.[1]	Number of Persons.
Exceeding. £	Not exceeding. £	£	
3,000	5000	55,868,841	14,463
5,000	10,000	67,221,053	9,847
10,000	15,000	31,123,363	2,579
15,000	20,000	18,625,572	1,084
20,000	25,000	13,535,953	606
25,000	30,000	8,861,139	326
30,000	40,000	11,331,470	330
40,000	50,000	7,350,334	163
50,000	75,000	9,885,783	161
75,000	100,000	5,954,713	69
100,000	. . .	17,498,903	95
Total , . . .		247,257,124	29,723

for the respective years will be approximately as follows " :

Year of Assessment.	Estimated total Income. £	Estimated yield of the Super-tax. £	Estimated No. of persons Chargeable.
1915–16	228,500,000	18,450,000	29,200
1916–17	258,600,000	21,400,000	31,760
1917–18	280,000,000	24,500,000	33,000

These estimates detract slightly from the surprising nature of the detailed tables, for

[1] See footnote on previous page.

6

they make the number of Super-Tax payers in 1916–17 larger and not smaller than in 1914–15 and they make the income nearly £14 millions instead of only £2½ millions higher. For the third war year they add further both to the number of Super-Tax-payers and to their aggregate income. Still the figures are enough to disprove completely the theories of the *Daily News* and *The Nation*, and when we allow for the increased Income Tax we shall find that the incomes of people with over £3,000 even as " expressed in money " have been lowered rather than raised by the war. Then we must reckon the further effect of the fall in the purchasing power of money in lowering the real value of all incomes. The *Economist* gives the following " Index Numbers " for the end of September, which we may take as the middle of each financial year.

These prices refer to commodities only, and

Year.				Index Number.
End September, 1913	.	.	.	123–3
„ 1914	.	.	.	126–4
„ 1915	.	.	.	151–6
„ 1916	.	.	.	201–0
„ 1917	.	.	.	256–1
„ 1918	.	.	.	283–1

a well-to-do man does not spend all his income on commodities ; still we cannot put the rise in the price of everything he may be expected to buy at less than 50 per cent. between September 1914 and September, 1916. This is the same thing as cutting down a given income by one-third.

Then we must make an allowance for the extra taxation, which has the same, but a more direct, result of lowering a nominal income. The Income Tax had been raised from the 1914–15 rate of 1s. 3d. (changed to 1s. 8d. in November, 1914) to 3s. for 1915–16 and 5s. for 1917–18, with proportionate additions to the Super Tax. We must use these figures, but they have not the same preciseness that they would have had before, say, 1904, for there has been no true Income Tax rate for many years past, since the rate of tax depends upon the amount of a man's income, perhaps one may say roughly that Super-Tax people paid 3s. in 1914–15, 4s. 6d. in 1915–16, and 6s. in 1916–17. If a further allowance be made for the fall in the purchasing power of money, which cannot be put lower than one-third for 1916–17, we get the following result showing the gross and net incomes of Super-Taxpayers in the three years beginning April 1st, 1914.

Year.	Gross Income. £	Less Income Tax. £	Rise in Prices. £	Net Income. £
1914–15 .	244 millions	36¼ millions	Nil	207½ millions
1915–16 .	225 ,,	50 ,,	29 millions	146 ,,
1916–17 .	247 ,,	76 ,,	57 ,,	114 ,,

In this table I have taken the incomes actually assessed ; if the estimate of the additional amounts to be secured finally be taken the figures are still remarkable but not quite so startling, and we get an estimate for 1917–18 as well.

Year.	Gross Income. £	Less Income Tax. £	Rise in Prices. £	Net Income. £
1914–15 .	244 millions	36½ millions	Nil	207½ millions
1915–16 .	228½ ,,	50⅔ ,,	29½ millions	148¼ ,,
1916–17 .	258 ,,	79¼ ,,	59⅜ ,,	119 ,,
1917–18 .	280 ,,	84 ,,	65 ,,	131 ,,

As a result of each year's war, therefore, we find that the real net income of the well-to-do classes has fallen steadily. Between 1914–15 and 1916–17 it may be said to have fallen by nearly two-fifths, *i.e.* from £207½ millions to either £114 millions or £119 millions, according to the table selected. These figures must not be taken as arithmetically precise, they are only deductions from approximate facts, and other calculators might work out different figures which would show either a smaller or a larger decline in the real income of the well-to-do classes ; but no one, not even the most hardened of expert witnesses in rating appeals, could use these figures to show anything except a considerable movement *against* people with over £3,000 a year.

What has really happened ? To give a complete answer one would need a detailed report upon the individual returns of the Super-Taxpayers, and such a report is out of the question. It may be surmised, however, that a considerable number of persons have dropped out of the Super Tax class owing to loss of income from one source or another. As Mr. Pethick Lawrence remarks in his Introduction[1] (page 13), " The total amount of national wealth and its distribution among the different classes of the nation suffers in war profound modification." Many capitalists, even those far below the £3,000 a year point, have their investments distributed over a wide area, some of them will have held

[1] *A Levy on Capital* (Allen & Unwin).

German or Austrian Government Stocks, or
Bulgarian " Sixes," or Turkish " Unified ",
and the Four per cents. of 1909. The income
from all these ceased sharply when war was
declared between England and each of the
four nations. The mere fact of war, too,
stopped the earning power of various other
investments ; property on the East Coast,
for instance, became almost valueless under
the menace of bombardment, and all over the
country the value of house property changed,
rising in one place and falling in another,
while cottage property fell in some areas and
was prevented from rising in the munition
areas by the Rent Restriction Act. Companies of all kinds, too, found great difficulty
in raising fresh capital, and many of them
suspended or reduced their dividends, rubber
companies, *e.g.* have been in difficulties ever
since the war began.

In saying this it is not necessary to deny
that war profits have been made, but it is
probable that not very much has been distributed in dividends. War profits, indeed,
have been made by individuals or by small
new companies rather than by large and old-
established concerns : thus farmers have

made large profits, especially in the earlier period of the war, but they do not come into the Super Tax list, and they are assessed to Income Tax on their rent, and not on their profits. Certain very big companies—Railways, Banks, and Gas Companies—reduced their dividends, the first two slightly and the last very seriously.

So far as we have gone there is no evidence that the propertied classes with over £3,000 a year have " made money out of the war." All the evidence in fact points to the conclusion that their incomes have been seriously reduced by the war. Let us in the next chapter see what has happened to their capital.

CHAPTER IX

CAPITAL CHANGES DURING THE WAR

THE editor of the *Daily News* asserts that " the capital of the individuals of the nation has increased during the war from £16,000 millions to £20,000 millions." This statement, or others in similar terms, forms the basis of the case for the Capital Levy. It seems so equitable to argue that " the propertied classes have added £4,000 millions to their wealth during the war, therefore they should be made to pay that sum to redeem the War Debt."

Granting for the moment that Mr. Gardiner's figures are accurate, what do they mean ? The pre-war capital was reckoned in gold pounds, the present capital is reckoned in paper pounds ; and a paper pound will now buy little more than one half as much as a gold pound would have bought five years ago Consequently, on Mr. Gardiner's figures, the *real* capital of the individuals of the nation has declined from £16,000 millions (gold) to £11,000 millions or £12,000 millions (gold). In short war has impoverished the nation, it has not enriched us; and that is exactly what the *Daily News* was arguing in July, 1914, and what we should expect to happen. It is one of the many disadvantages of a Government paper currency un-supported by gold that all comparisons with the conditions which prevailed under the gold standard are subject to an indefinite percentage of error. A currency such as we have at present is almost bound to depreciate continually; in other countries, such as Russia, we can see the process of depreciation 'at work because it has been so rapid; in our own case it' is not so easy to perceive it, just as a member of a family hardly notices how the others are growing older because the change from day to day is imperceptible.

Perhaps the popular belief in the money-making power of war would not be so strong if people would think out what is meant by the national capital. Stocks and shares and bonds and certificates and deeds are not " capital," they are only evidences of title to capital. The national capital is to be found in railways, houses, factories, harbours, rolling stock, cattle, stock-in-trade, and so on. Is it not clear that the war has not extended our railways, or improved their permanent way, or increased their rolling stock? It has, in fact, done precisely the opposite in each case, rolling stock has been exported and not replaced, repairs and renewals have been postponed, rails have actually been torn up and sent to France. So, too, with houses, new ones have not been built, and we are faced with a shortage reckoned by hundreds of thousands; old houses have been allowed to fall into disrepair. It is the same with other kinds of property, everyone knows how our cattle and pigs and sheep and horses have diminished in numbers and how the stock-in-trade of every business has been cut down until every trader lives from hand to mouth. Factories alone have increased greatly in size and number, but the new factories have been built mainly for the manufacture of war material; they are seldom planned with a view to their use in peace time, and their after-war value may prove to be very small. Our mercantile marine, too, has been destroyed at an alarming rate, and although from the shipowners' point of view the destruction makes little difference, since it has raised the value of his remaining vessels enormously, from a national point of view each ship sunk is a loss of capital. On the Continent there has been a deliberate destruction of capital, not only of buildings and railways but even the very soil has been rendered sterile over large areas, dug up, buried, impregnated with poison.

The national " capital," in the, sense of commodities, machinery, plant, and so on has undoubtedly been lessened by the war ; yet at the same time the amount of stocks, bonds, shares and certificates has grown. The result of these two processes, *i.e.* the destruction of capital and the creation of " paper wealth " is that each paper unit represents a smaller share of the aggregate wealth. Consequently a man who was " worth," as we say, £10,000 before the war, supposing that he has made no change in his investments, is no longer worth £10,000, but something like £7,500 if he held " gilt-edged " securities, such as Consols, Municipal Loans, or debentures in sound companies. If he

held agricultural land or shares in industrial
companies he is probably worth more than
£10,000 ; if he owned ships or coal he may
be worth £15,000 ; if he was a dairy farmer
and has maintained his herd of cows in un-
diminished numbers and condition he is probably worth £20,000. But the farmer is
seldom a large capitalist, and the man with
over £2,000 worth of cows is unusual. Individuals owning ships are still more rare,
and although great landowners who are also
colliery proprietors may be met occasionally,
most large commercial undertakings are now
worked by limited companies. It will be
found that most Stock Exchange securities
have fallen in price since July, 1914, and the
few instances to the contrary, such as shipping or armament shares, represent a small
fraction of the whole. Even if the change in
market prices had moved in the opposite
direction, so that most stocks showed a rise
instead of a fall in price, the real result would
still mean a loss to holders unless the percentage of rise was enough to counterbalance
the depreciation of the currency. For this
purpose a stock worth £100 in July, 1914,
would have to rise to something between

£150 and £180; whereas, in fact, a gilt-edged stock worth £100 in July, 1914, is only worth about £75 in November, 1918.

It is possible to show the precise effect of the war on investment stocks, because the *Bankers' Magazine* publishes at intervals of a month or two a list of 387 selected securities with their market values on the Stock Exchange. Before the war these 387 stocks were valued at £3,370 millions (gold) on July 20th, 1914. By December, 1917, they had sunk to £2,600 millions (paper). With the successive offensives which broke the Hindenburg Line in the summer and autumn of 1918, followed by the capitulation of Bulgaria and the German appeal for an armistice, prices rallied from their lowest point, and the list published as I write shows that on October 18th the aggregate value had recovered to £2,794 millions (paper), showing a decline of £576 millions. This table is interesting enough to be reproduced in full.

Nominal Amount (Par Value).	Department, containing	July 20, 1914.	October 18, 1918.	Increase or Decrease.
£		£	£	£
862,768	9 British and Indian	690,355	565,650	− 124,705
52,250	7 Corporation (U.K.)	45,812	36,574	− 9,238
82,850	11 Colonial Government . . .	79,288	71,435	− 7,858
18,250	10 Corporation Stocks (Col. & For.) .	16,479	13,944	− 2,535
881,950	31 Foreign Govt.	746,677	555,447	− 191,230
310,750	26 Brit. Rail. Ord. .	269,513	204,994	− 64,519
133,500	11 „ Deb. .	116,066	88,124	− 27,942
149,500	13 „ Pref. .	128,168	94,325	− 33,843
26,000	5 Indian Railway .	25,366	20,801	− 4,565
88,440	9 Railways British Possessions .	83,686	70,313	− 13,373
346,000	17 American Railways	346,085	274 202	− 71,883
178 000	16 „ Bonds (Gold)	167,425	149,830	− 17,595
63,940	24 Foreign Railways	58,645	43,278	− 15,367
29,338	14 British Banks	182,650	171,446	− 11,204
10,175	9 Colonial Banks .	20,657	21,576	+ 919
15,420	13 Semi - Foreign Banks . .	34,958	36,315	+ 1,357
15,900	18 Brewery Stocks .	20,040	20,237	+ 197
9,000	4 Canals and Docks	5,040	5,282	+ 242
36,701	38 Commercial and Industrial . .	81,662	82,353	+ 691
3,180	6 Electric Light and Power . .	4,021	3,264	− 757
7,120	11 Land and Investment . . .	21,537	20,785	− 752
28,635	5 Gas . . .	33,290	23,745	− 9,545
5,390	21 Insurance . .	40,606	45,683	+ 5,077
11,910	8 Iron, Coal, & Steel	20,796	24,709	+ 3,913
7,200	7 Shipping . .	14,546	25,522	+ 10,976
8,885	4 Telegraphs and Telephones .	10,542	12,712	+ 1,630
4,970	7 Tramways and Omnibus . .	5,516	4,887	− 629
2 715	4 Waterworks .	2,854	2,454	− 400
20,704	15 S African Mines .	55,458	51,705	− 3,753
9,703	6 Copper . .	41,208	50,823	+ 9,615
3,424	8 Miscel. Mining .	1,763	2,667	+ 904
3,424,856	387 Totals . .	3,370,709	2,794,542	− 576,167

Some Stocks, it will be seen, have risen in price, but these are mainly " speculative " securities, such as copper and shipping shares, things which a stockbroker does not recommend to the cautious or small investor. In the case of British Railways, taking debenture, preference and ordinary stocks, the fall is one of £126 millions from a pre-war level of £513 millions, or nearly one quarter. We may work out the real loss as follows, the figures being submitted merely as an estimate:

		£
Pre-war market price . . (1)		3,370,709,000
October 18, 1918 . . (2)		2,794,542,000
Loss in market price . (3)		576,167,000
Add to loss one-third of (2) for fall in value of money (4)		931,514,000
Total loss in 4⅓ years of war . =		1,507,681,000

Since the few rises in market price are to be found among the more speculative Stocks we may reckon quite roughly, but with little fear of contradiction, that gilt-edged fixed-interest-yielding Stocks have lost nearly one half of their real value through the war. The war has been paid for by *a concealed Levy* on certain kinds of property. The owners still hold their property, it looks the same and bears the same figures, but its real value has been halved. The documents of title to shares in the national wealth have been multiplied, but the wealth itself has been diminished, consequently each old document represents a smaller share than it did four and a half years ago. As each successive War Loan has been floated, or even as the daily output of War Bonds has continued, holders of Consols, of Municipal Loan Stocks, or of debentures and prior charges in companies, have lost fraction after fraction of their claim on the national output after the war.

Before the war, moreover, Englishmen held documents—foreign war Stocks, shares in foreign railways and other remunerative undertakings—which entitled them to receive so many million pounds a year for interest or dividends. These millions came, of course, not in money but in goods and services rendered to us by the foreigner. This stream of goods and services seems likely to change its course and to flow westwards across the Atlantic, though a smaller current should set in towards our shores from our debtors on the Continent unless this is counteracted, as it may be, by the claims of the neutral countries, which have been buying back their securities from us and have bought some of our own securities too. If this is so, there will be prior claims on the national output which will reduce still further the share available for the owners of pre-war wealth.

It is, I hope, unnecessary to deal further with the allegation that the propertied classes " have made money out of the war." It has been made as plain as figures can make it that most kinds of property have depreciated from 30 to 60 per cent as a direct result of the war, and of the method adapted in 1914–15 for financing it. These calculations are based on the fact, which is not, I think, denied by anyone, that the measure of value itself, *i.e.* the pound sterling, has changed. We have reached the extraordinary position that no one knows exactly what the pound sterling is worth; for many years past Englishmen have boasted that their sovereign was the best known coin in the world, circulating in all civilised and some other countries at its full value. Now we have " sovereigns " in paper, printed and issued every week, until

7

there are no less than £287 millions of paper pounds supported by a mere £28½ millions of gold—the same amount of gold as when the note issue was only £46½ millions—in June, 1915.

It is not the purpose of this book to discuss currency questions, but the issue and over-issue of Treasury Notes has had a marked and deplorable effect in increasing the money cost of the war and possibly its real cost as well. The evils of a Government Note issue were recognised long before the war. Mr. Huth Jackson, in his presidential address to the Institute of Bankers in November, 1910, quoted the well-known American authority, Mr. Conant, who wrote in his *History of Modern Banks* as follows :

" A Government paper currency has rarely been issued to promote the convenience of commerce, and has seldom contributed to that end. Experience, as well as theory, has proved that Government paper money is essentially different in character from banking paper, and opens a Pandora's box of evil for every nation which uses it. The difference between a Government paper currency and bank notes is not one of experience or accident merely ; it is a difference which is fundamental. Banking paper is based on business transactions, and is limited by their demands; Government paper is based upon the will of the State, and is limited only by its necessities. The almost invariable rule of Government paper issues is that one begets another, until the entire volume exceeds the legitimate demands of business, upsets values, and goes beyond the reach of restriction of the metallic standard. . . . Even a limited issue of paper is maintained at par by a Government with much greater difficulty than by a well regulated bank. The reason is fundamental. The Government has no quick assets. It is not wealth in the abstract that currency must represent, but quickly negotiable wealth. The Government has only two resources (beyond the cash in hand)—the pledge of public property and the power of taxation. The peculiar strength of a banking currency lies in the enormous mass of quick assets behind its demand liabilities."

This dictum, endorsed by the Nestor of economists and bankers—Sir R. H. Inglis Palgrave, F.R.S., was quoted in the report which I helped to present to the Economic section at the Manchester meeting of the British Association in September, 1915. Even at that early date our Committee felt alarmed at the continuous increase in the amount of the note issue, although it was then only £54½ millions, and we suggested their gradual withdrawal and the issue of £1 and 10s. notes by the Bank of England to take their place.[1]

In the current number of the *Economic Journal* (September, 1918), Dr. J. C. Stamp, whose work on *British Incomes and Property* (1916), makes him one of the leading authorities on the subject and possibly the first among them, conducts a careful inquiry into the pre-war and post-war wealth of individuals in the United Kingdom. He comes to the conclusion that " the capital in private hands which would have been returnable in practice for Capital Levy before the war could not have exceeded £11,500 millions or have been less than £10,500 millions." In estimating the post-war capital, Dr. Stamp admits that the data are far less certain : he reckons that the rate of investment interest will remain

[1] The "first interim report" of the Committee on Currency and Foreign Exchanges after the War, which was published on October 30th, 1918, take the same view. Lord Cunliffe and his colleagues, among whom are Lord Inchcape and the Secretary to the Treasury, Sir John Bradbury, declare unanimously that "it is, in our judgment, imperative that the issue of fiduciary notes shall be, as soon as practicable, once more limited by law"; and they add, almost in the words of the British Association report, "we recommend that the Note Issue (except as regards existing private issues) should be entirely in the hands of the Bank of England." . . . "the outstanding Currency Notes should be retired and Bank of England notes of low denomination substituted."

near its present level of 5 per cent, and that prices will be about 25 per cent higher than before the war. He works out the following additions to and reduction in pre-war wealth:

Additions

	£
Agricultural land . . .	250,000,000
Farmers' capital . . .	100,000,000
Goodwill	50,000,000
Houses and trade buildings .	350,000,000
„ new . . .	100,000,000
War Loans, etc. . . .	5,000,000,000
Moveable property not yielding Income (furniture, etc.)	400,000,000
Total . . .	6,250,000,000

Less Reductions

Foreign investments sold .	800,000,000
Depreciation of railways .	200,000,000
Net addition . . .	5,200,000,000

Thus Dr. Stamp brings the capital wealth of the United Kingdom in private hands as at March, 1919, to " the neighbourhood of £16,000 millions." It will be noticed that he takes no account of the fall in the buying power of money, as that question lies outside his investigation.

If, then, we apply our deduction of one-third for depreciation of the currency, we get the following result :

			£
Post-war valuation	.	.	16,000,000,000
Deduct one-third	.	.	5,333,000,000
Result	.	.	10,667,000,000

The war, with its huge Loans and apparently vast additions to the capital of individuals, is seen to have reduced their real capital. Since we are talking of capital and not of income the question of Income Tax does not arise, but we must not forget that the owners of post-war capital will have to bear the burden of a War Income Tax for the rest of their lives.

CHAPTER X

INCOME CHANGES DURING THE WAR

OUR last chapter discussed changes in the distribution of wealth during the war, and led 'to the conclusion that the pre-war owners of capital were, on the average, poorer than when the war began, in spite of the War Loan Stock which they may be assumed to hold. We must now enquire what changes the war has made in the distribution of the national income.

The Inland Revenue Report already quoted gives a certain amount of information, but much less than the corresponding reports for pre-war years; in fact it has only twenty-two pages, as compared with the 160 pages of the 1914–15 report. We have seen how little of the increased money income went to persons with over £3,000 a year: unfortunately there are no precisely parallel figures for incomes below the Super Tax level. The chief figure is that called " Gross income

brought under the review of the Department,"
which was £1,167⅙ millions for 1913–14 and
£1,662¾ millions for 1916–17, showing an
apparent growth in the incomes of the Income
Tax Paying classes of £495 millions. But
here the comparison is upset because the
things compared are not the same, since in
the first year the point of total exemption
from Income Tax was £160 a year, while in
the second year it was £130; so we must
make an allowance for the incomes between
those two points which are included in the
1916–17 total. A further allowance must be
made for Farmers' Profits (Schedule B),
since the basis was changed by Mr. McKenna
from one-third of the rent to the whole rent,
so that the gross total rose from £17½ millions
in the earlier year to £51½ millions in the later
year. Perhaps the farmers' figures ought to
be excluded from our calculations altogether,
since they are not based upon profits or
income at all and may have little relation to
either. One of the most obvious reforms in
Income Tax law would be to assess farmers
on their real profits.

After " Gross Income " we have another
figure called " Taxable Income," which is

obtained by striking out (1) " that fraction of
the income of exempt persons which comes
under the provision of the Department " ;
(2) incomes of charities, hospitals, etc., and
(3) allowances, repairs, etc. " Taxable Income," therefore, is the net income of taxable
persons. The figures for 1913–14 and 1916–17
are £951 millions and £1,373½ millions re-
spectively. Next we come to the third and
final figure, " Income on which Tax was
received "—*i.e.* Taxable Income, less abatements, life insurance premium, and relief for
children. This total for the two years is
£791¾ millions and £981¾ millions, showing a
growth of £190 millions only. In spite of the
lowered abatements, the amounts allowed
show the large growth from £159½ millions to
£311½ millions. This seems to indicate a
correspondingly large growth in the number
of smaller incomes. It may be well to set out
these figures in tabular form :

	1913–14. £	1916–17. £
(a) " Gross Income ".	1,167,184,000	1,662,724,000
(b) Allowances, etc.	216,143,700	289,272,200
(c) " Taxable Income "	951,040,000	1,373,451,000
(d) Abatements, etc.	159,325,600	391,735,900
(e) " Income on which Tax was received "	791,714,000	981,715,000

	1913–14.	1916–17.
	£	£
(f) Total net produce of Tax	43,523,000	201,636,000
Net produce per penny .	3,108,000	3,360,000
Average effective rate of Tax on each pound of Taxable Income . .	Tax, 1s. 2d.	2s. 11d. (Tax, 5s. in £1.)

There is little in this table to suggest any large addition to the incomes of persons above the limit of abatement, *i.e.* £700 a year, indeed the immense growth in the amount allowed for the reduced abatements suggests very forcibly that the growth is to be found in the smaller incomes, *i.e.* those which get larger, abatements.

If we allow £150,000,000 for the new class of taxpayer, *i.e.* those with incomes between £130 and £160 a year, £34 millions for the treble assessment of farmers, and £20 millions for the extra share of super-tax people, we get £495–£204, *i.e.* £291 millions as the extra income received by persons with incomes between £160 and £3,000 a year.

It would not be fair, however, to treat this sum as the increased incomes of those who were paying Income Tax before the war, because a huge army of Government employees, skilled workmen, and others, have had war bonuses and war wages which have brought them well above the £160 a year point. In fact, it looks very much as if a large number of pre-war Income Tax Payers have dropped out of the class altogether ; perhaps this may be explained by the enlistment of so many thousands in the Army. It is one of the anomalies, and perhaps the most indefensible one, of military service, that a man who does the most vital and dangerous work for the State gets the smallest pay of any kind of worker.

Our table gives something like the net incomes of the Income Tax Paying class if we deduct (f) from (c), which gives a total of £1,171¾ millions, but from this again we must take £140 millions for persons with incomes between £130 and £160, and £164 millions a year for the net income of Super Tax Payers. Finally, in order to shew the effect of the war, we must subtract from the last-mentioned total one-third, in order to allow for the lessened purchasing power of money :

	1913–14.		1916–17.	
	£		£	
Net Income .	907½ millions.	Net Income .	867¾ millions
Less Super				
Tax Payers.	210 ,,	Less one-third	289 ,,
	697½ ,,		578¾ ,,

It is surely clear from these figures, which are based upon the only available statistics, that the real income of the propertied or Income Tax Paying classes has diminished very seriously as a result of the war. Moreover, as was demonstrated in an earlier chapter, the money income of the nation has increased enormously as the result of Government expenditure out of borrowed money. If the Government had pursued the sound policy of paying its way by taxation there would have been no increase in the money income of the nation, because what the Government spent would be obtained from the taxpayer. Had that method been adopted it would be clear to the meanest capacity that the well-to-do classes were paying for the war, because through the Income Tax they would have been contributing the greater part of the revenue which the Government would be distributing in wages, pay, allowances and pensions. Nevertheless, the propertied classes would really have been much better off even if the Income Tax had been graduated from 5s. to 15s. in the pound as soon as the war started, for the diminished income which was left to them would have maintained its purchasing power, and, when the war was over, they could look forward to an immediate reduction in taxation and would not have to face the burden of an enormous War Debt.

It is not necessary to argue that every penny which is spent on a war should be raised by taxation; it is sufficient for my purpose to affirm that all money required for pay, wages, allowances and pensions, shall be obtained by taxation and not by borrowing. If the Government has to buy land, houses or ships, it may pay for these things out of loans, for they are what is called "capital expenditure." One of the chief purposes of money or currency is to act as machinery for moving commodities from the persons who produce them to the persons who consume them. In War-time there are not so many commodities available as at other times, therefore less money or currency is needed to move them; yet our Government has nearly doubled the amount of money, whether by "Money" we mean income or currency. Lord Cunliffe's Committee, whose Report[1] is published as I write this chapter (November 2nd), reckons that the amount of legal tender money ex-

[1] Cd. 9182. Committee on Currency and Foreign Exchanges after the War.

panded from £180 millions on June 30th, 1914, to £282¾ millions on July 10th, 1918; £29 millions of currency notes have since been added to the latter total. Roughly, we have £20 now to do less work than £9 did four-and-half years ago! According to the " Quantitative Theory " of money, prices should be rather more than double those of July, 1914.

On an earlier page it was suggested that the money income of the country had increased from £2,400 to £3,600 millions. Since there are no statistics of incomes under £130 a year, and since it is not clear how far the increases of weekly wage-earners are included in the Inland Revenue return, estimates of the present national income must be vague; the following may be put forward as a guess :

	£
Incomes of 1913–14 . . .	2,400,000,000
Deduct for War Loss (one-eighth)	300,000,000
	2,100,000,000
Add for Government expenditure in United Kingdom (including that of Dominions and Allies) .	1,800,000,000
	3,900,000,000
Deduct for Excess Profits Duty .	300,000,000
Net Income	3,600,000,000

It will at once be asked : " Where have the
£3,600 millions gone ? if only £1,662 millions
come within the purview of Somerset House
and only £1,373 millions were taxable ? " In
1913–14 Somerset House took cognisance of
£1,167 millions only, yet the Treasury
reckoned the national income at £2,400
millions, or more than twice as much. At
first sight one would expect to find a larger
proportion of the national income passing
through the Inland Revenue statistics, since
there are all the incomes between £130 and
£160 which now pay Income Tax for the first
time, and all those whose incomes have been
raised substantially, say from £100 to £150 or
£200 a year. In the absence of any mention
of wage-earners in the Inland Revenue return
one must infer that there has been a serious,
perhaps an immense leakage. No doubt it
takes time for the Inland Revenue officials,
with a much depleted staff, to bring the new
machinery of quarterly assessments into
efficient working. The quarterly assessment
of wage-earners was an unhappy device ; if
the wage-earner was to pay Income Tax he
should have paid it weekly, just as he pays
his threepence or fourpence under the National

Insurance Act. Had that Act been based on quarterly payments the friction and loss would have been enormous. Perhaps a part of the apparent discrepancy may be accounted for by the hundreds of thousands of women workers who have come into industry to take men's places and who are getting good wages, *e.g.* £2 a week, for the first time.

In any case, it seems certain that by far the larger part of the increased money income of the nation since August, 1914, has gone to the wage-earners. The old distinction between Income Tax Payers and wage-earners has disappeared, partly as a result of Mr. McKenna's Budgets, but more as a result of the immense rise in wages. It is quite possible that whereas the wage-earners were getting say one-half of the national income before the war, or £1,200 millions a year, they are now getting two-thirds, or £2,400 millions; their share cannot be put lower than three-fifths (or £2,160 millions) at the lowest estimate. These are gross figures; in order to find net incomes one must deduct some £500 or £600 millions for taxation, less £50 or £60 millions, for that amazingly foolish thing the Loaf Subsidy.

This might work out more or less as follows :

	Share of Wage-earners. £	Share of the Rest. £
Income . .	2,400,000,000	1,200,000,000
Less taxation .	150,000,000	350,000,000
Net Income .	2,250,000,000	850,000,000

Or taking the three-fifths and two-fifths divisions, we have :

	Share of Wage-earners. £	Share of the Rest. £
Income . .	2,160,000,000	1,440,000,000
Less taxation .	130,000,000	370,000,000
Net Income .	2,030,000,000	1,070,000,000

In conclusion : it should now be evident that the War Debt has been incurred, mainly, in order to pay inflated rates to the wage-earners, not to pay inflated profits to the owners of property. A general increase in the rate of wages was overdue before the war, especially in the case of the agricultural labourer and of country workers as a whole : it is unfortunate that this increase should have required a war in order to bring it about. During the four years and a half of war there has been a shifting of incomes, and of capital as well, from

8

the pre-war capitalist class to the wage-earning class. Since the war wages have been paid mainly out of War Loans, and since these Loans were largely a concealed Levy on pre-war capital, the wage-earners have had a wonderful opportunity of becoming capitalists themselves. Many of them have saved, as the records of War Savings Associations prove : if a larger number preferred to spend freely and force up prices, while others saved their better wages (which were exempt from the Excess Profits Duty), they have no one to blame but themselves.

Soon after this chapter was written, the Committee on Financial Facilities (with Sir R. Vassar Smith as Chairman and the Secretary to the Treasury, Sir John Bradbury, among his colleagues) published its Report (Cd. 9227). The Committee comes to the same conclusions as those reached by Lord Cunliffe's Committee. It says "there is no legal limit to the amount of Currency Notes which may be issued, and there is, therefore, no automatic check upon the expansion of credit. The total deposits of the Banks of the United Kingdom (other than the Bank of England) which amounted on the 31st December, 1913, to £1,070,000,000 are now approaching £2,000,000,000. These figures are an indication of the very great expansion of credit which has taken place up to the present time, and which still remains unchecked. The enormously increased purchasing power thus created has, in our opinion, been one of the main factors contributing to the rise in prices which has taken place."

On December 24th, 1918, the total issue of Currency Notes and Certificates amounted to £323,644,400, so that the ratio of gold to notes has fallen to 8·8 per cent !

CHAPTER XI

FURTHER CONSIDERATIONS ON THE
CAPITAL LEVY

IF it be proved, as seems sufficiently clear, that the propertied classes have not " made money out of the war," but are, on the contrary, very much poorer as a result of it, are there still any arguments in support of a Capital Levy on them in order to pay off the War Debt. Mr. Bonar Law told the Trade Unionist Deputation, introduced by Mr. Sidney Webb (November 14th, 1917), that " the question of whether or not there should be conscription of wealth is entirely a matter of expediency, which concerns mainly not the working classes but the people who have money." It is deplorable that a Chancellor of the Exchequer should use so vague a phrase as " people who have money." Taken literally it is a truism, for a pauper obviously cannot pay either a levy

or a tax ; but in this sense it should not be
used in contrast with " the working classes,"
since there is no class nowadays, except the
aged and disabled, which does not work,
and if Mr. Law means wage-earners, as no
doubt he does, his assumption is unfounded
because, as we have seen, the wage-earners
in the aggregate have had far more money
to spend than the rest of the community. If,
again, Mr. Law means persons with large
incomes, *e.g.* over £3,000 a year, his statement
is still untrue, since these incomes are not
all derived from property, probably not even
the majority of them, for they include the
salaries of Cabinet Ministers and Judges, who
show a regrettable disinclination to serve
their country for naught.

The whole income of the Super Tax class
was only estimated at £280 millions for
1917–18, and from this total the sum of
£94½ millions was extracted for Income and
Super Tax. At the present time (1918–19)
the proportion extracted by taxation has
risen from one-third to more than two-fifths.
If the whole of the remainder were confis-
cated, which is inconceivable, it would not
pay more than half the interest on the War

Debt. As we go lower down the list of incomes the proportion derived from earnings becomes constantly higher.

Taking Dr. Stamp's figure of £16,000 millions for the total value of privately-owned property we may calculate the income from it as about £880 millions a year. This is less than a quarter of the suggested total for the national income (£3,600 millions), so that there is all the difference in the world for " the people who have money " between payment by Levy and payment by Tax. In the case of a Levy the burden would fall upon the owners of the £880 millions and mainly, if graduated, on those who owned about half of it ; in the case of a Tax, the burden would fall on the owners of the £3,600 millions and again, if graduated, mainly on those who own about half of it, among whom the owners of the £880 millions would pay a heavier percentage than the rest. Is any further argument needed to prove the unfairness of the proposed Capital Levy ?

There are still, I believe, some people who think that the alternative after the war is between a Capital Levy and a high Income Tax ; they reckon that if there is a Levy they will pay it " once and for all " and start free from all worry about the War Debt. They take Mr. Bonar Law's view that it does not much matter which they pay—the Levy now or the Tax for the rest of their lives. Mr. Pethick Lawrence elaborates this contention in his book, *A Levy on Capital.* He says " A very high Income Tax would hit them at least as hard, and in some ways would be more objectionable " (page 66), and later he argues that a Levy would enable the Income Tax rate to be lowered from 7s. 6d. in the £ to 3s. 6d. There are two answers to this contention, one being that the figures are wrong and the other that the protagonists of the Capital Levy have no intention of letting the rate of Income Tax be lowered.

On the first point I may quote Professor Scott (*Economic Journal,* September, 1918, page 256) : " If the Levy is to be a straight deal and not a crooked one, it must take at least as much as the capitalised value of the taxes it commutes : it is likely to take more both directly and indirectly. Therefore *a fortiori* if the country can bear the Levy it could bear the taxation for which it is to be substituted." Or one may say—suppose that

a certain sum must be raised by Income Tax ;
after a graduated Levy the larger revenues
would be greatly reduced. They could only be
taxed on the reduced income, and so rates
would have to rise much more steeply than
at present, the maximum being reached at a
much smaller income. Already Super Tax
people, under the 1918–19 Budget pay about
eight shillings in the £ of their aggregate
income, and the graduated Levy would be
paid largely by these people, many of whom
would drop out of the Super Tax class altogether.

Taxation of the bigger incomes has become
so high that every millionaire has a Senior
Partner—the Chancellor of the Exchequer.
Leaseholders in Belgravia imagine that they
are paying rent to the Duke of Westminster ;
they are mistaken, Mr. Bonar Law takes the
larger share.

What would happen under Mr. Lawrence's
proposal is simply that the property owner,
who may have quite a moderate income of
£1,000 or £2,000, would be taxed out of
existence in order that the Income Tax paid
by Cabinet Ministers and Judges might be
lowered. Moreover since the income from

property is only one quarter of the national income, the property owner would have to give up nearly £20,000 in order to lower the Cabinet Minister's Income Tax by a shilling in the pound. Perhaps there is not much driving power behind the proposal to reduce the Cabinet Minister's Income Tax; so I come to the second point—that a Levy would not be allowed to reduce the rate of Income Tax.

Here I may quote the official resolutions of the Socialist and Labour Parties. At the Leicester Conference of the Independent Labour Party the official resolution ran as follows :

" This Conference considers that the most equitable method of wiping out the National Debt and of securing a redistribution of wealth is the adoption of a system of progressive taxation or appropriation by the community of all capital values owned by individuals, together with the graduated taxation of all incomes above an agreed minimum. The Conference therefore declares that a graduated tax should be imposed on capital wealth commencing at 5 per cent. on £2,000 valuation, and rising by proportionate graduation to 33⅓ per cent. on £1,000,000 and over, together with a steeply graduated tax imposed on all incomes, the tax rising to 18s. in the £ in the case of huge incomes so as to secure the ultimate extinguishing of all unearned increment."

Mr. F. W. Jowett, M.P., in seconding the resolution, made it clear that the Levy was only to apply to a small minority of capitalists: " There must," he said, " be a minimum fixed that will leave the working class investor free from penalisation." He added that the funds, often large, of Trade Unions, or of Co-operative and Friendly Societies must also be exempted.

The Labour Party, at its Westminster Conference, June 26–28th, 1918, had a milder and more general resolution which reads as follows :

" 1. That in view of the enormous debts contracted during the war, and of the necessity to lighten national financial burdens in order to enable the country to compete successfully on the markets of the world so soon as peace comes, this Conference demands that an equitable system of conscription of accumulated wealth should be put into operation forthwith, with exemption for fortunes below £1,000, and a graduated scale of rates for larger totals, believing that no system of taxation only of income or profits will yield enough to free the country from oppressive debts, and that any attempt to tax food

or the other necessities of life would be unjust and
ruinous to the masses of the people.

" 2. That the only solution of the difficulties that
have arisen is a system by which the necessary
national income shall be derived mainly from direct
taxation alike of land and accumulated wealth, and
of income and profits, together with suitable imposts
upon luxuries, and that the death duties and the
taxation upon unearned incomes should be substantially increased and equitably regraded."

The Labour Party is a larger and more
composite body than the I.L.P., and likes a
certain vagueness about its resolutions ; but
the second part points clearly enough to the
continuance of a high Income Tax. There is
no suggestion that the Levy should be used
to lower the rate of Tax beyond the assertion
that Income Tax and Excess Profits Duty
combined are insufficient to pay off the War
Debts. In fact, the demand for a repeal of
the food taxes points to higher rate of direct
taxation.

It may escape notice on a first reading, but
a second perusal will show that the Labour
Party proposes to tax the same things three
times. Property, or " accumulated wealth "
or " unearned income " is to suffer: (1) a
Capital Levy, (2) extra direct taxation, and (3)

a specially high Income Tax rate. Apparently the Labour Party wishes not only to (1) eat its cake and (2) have it too, but also (3) to give it away ; or, to vary the metaphor, it will kill the goose which lays the golden eggs and then rear a nice brood of golden goslings.

In the election manifesto published by the Labour Party on November 28th these proposals were given a more popular form :

" In paying the War Debt, Labour will place the burden on the broadest backs by a special tax on capital. Those who have made fortunes out of the war must pay for the war; and Labour will insist upon heavily graduated direct taxation with a raising of the exemption limit. This is what Labour means by the conscription of wealth."

The *Manchester Guardian's* expert on this matter, whose identity is thinly concealed behind the initials J. A. H., goes out of his way (January 21st, 1918) to confound those of his critics who appeared to think that his " Case for a Capital Levy " was proposed as a substitute for a high Income Tax. " No such thing," (he writes). " If my proposal were carried out there would still remain the need for an Income and a Super Tax on a higher level than the present ones."

CHAPTER XII

THE ALTERNATIVE

TO dismiss the Capital Levy as impracticable and unjust is not sufficient unless one can also put forward an alternative scheme which will set our national finances on a sound basis after the war.

In the earlier part of this book I discussed the rise in prices, and showed that it was an inevitable result of the increased money income in the hands of the public. This increased income was itself caused by the Government's distribution of hundreds of millions which it had borrowed or had created by inflation. We saw, accordingly, that people might have much more money than they had a year earlier and yet be no better off. There was, it is true, *a more equal* distribution of income, because the borrowed money was spent mainly in wages, but the country as a whole was no richer. Is it not conceivable that there may be a converse of this proposition, *i.e.* that the country as a whole may have less money income and yet be no poorer ?

Under a financial system such as prevailed in most countries, except our own, before the war ; *i.e.* one which depends for national revenue mainly upon indirect taxation (tea, sugar, wheat, beer, or tobacco duties), an increase in taxation means an increase in the disparity between rich and poor, because such taxation checks the poor man's consumption and has little effect on the rich man. But an Income Tax, if graduated as the British Income Tax is graduated, means a lessened disparity between rich and poor, because the rich man pays heavily and the poor man pays at a much lower rate, or perhaps nothing at all. Let us imagine four classes, each having the same gross income, and then see the effect of a graduated Income Tax on their share of the net income :

	Number,	Income of each. £	Taxation. £	Net Income. £
(a)	1,000	100	0	100,000
(b)	100	1,000	20,000	80,000
(c)	10	10,000	30,000	70,000
(d)	1	100,000	50,000	50,000
		Total	100,000	300,000

The result of the taxation is that class (a)—
the poorest—gets one-third of the net income,
which amounts to the same thing as if there
had been no taxation and class (a) had
received an extra £50,000. Something of this
kind has actually happened during the war,
only the wage-earners have received their
extra £50,000 while the wealthier classes have
been paying their £100,000 in Income and
Super Tax.

The alternative to a Capital Levy is a
Reformed Income Tax. If my theory that
prices are merely a relation between money
and commodities is a sound one, there should
be no difficulty about raising any required
amount of revenue by an Income Tax. This
theory maintains that as the Income Tax
rises, provided it is paid by all citizens above
the poverty line, prices fall. With a perfectly
adjusted system the Income Tax would be
indefinitely elastic, and could raise any sum
which might be necessary. Fortunately, our
requirements are not infinite, and do not call
for an excessive share of the national income.
Let us first construct a post-war Budget :

	£
Interest on War Debt . .	400,000,000
Sinking Fund . . .	40,000,000
Pensions	60,000,000
Ordinary Expenditure, with additions	250,000,000
	750,000,000

On the revenue side we must allow for the disappearance of the Excess Profits Duty, since it is essentially a tax on war profits, and these must be deemed to end when peace comes. This will mean a serious inroad into the revenue system of the 1918–19 Budget, but it should be accompanied by an addition to the receipts from Income Tax, since the Duty was applied, in practice to profits which had nothing to do with the war, such as those of the younger rubber companies, which are sometimes paying the Duty though they are not paying a dividend. The existing taxes, minus the Excess Profits Duty, might work out as follows :

	1918–19. £	1919–20. £
Customs .	94·5 millions.	106 millions.
Excise . .	53·2 ,,	60 ,,
Income and Super-tax .	290·4 ,,	350 ,,

	1918–19.		1919–20.	
	£		£	
Miscellaneous	25·1	millions.	25	millions.
Stamps . .	9·2	,,	9	,,
Estate Duties	31·5	,,	32	,,
Profits of Post Office .	8·0	,,	8	,,
	512·0	,,	590	,,

There is thus a gap of £160 millions, which, apparently, must be filled almost entirely by an increased rise from Income Tax. A certain amount of additional revenue may be obtained from some of the smaller taxes, thus the absurd tobacconist's license of 5s. 3d. a year should be graduated according to the rateable value of the premises, *e.g.* 10s. 6d. for premises over £25 a year, £1 1s. over £50, and another £1 1s. for each £50 of rateable value up, say, to a maximum of £21 for premises of £1,000 and over. Dog licenses should be raised to 10s. 6d. Motor vehicles of *all* kinds should be taxed according to a combination of weight and horse-power: at present a lorry weighing over five tons pays 15s., or £3 3s. less than one of 4½ tons ! The license duty on menservants might be graduated, *e.g.* £1 1s. for the first, £2 2s. for the second, and £3 3s. for each additional servant.

My proposal for a tax on cinemas (*Contemporary Review*, December, 1914) was carried into effect by Mr. McKenna in his 1916 Budget, but there is much to be said for an additional license fee both on cinemas and on music halls or variety theatres. The petrol duty should be maintained at a high figure, since motor vehicles wear out our roads, impose a heavy burden on the ratepayer, and drive him and his childrenꞁoff the so-called King's Highway. When the numerable restrictions on sales and consumption and importation and exportation are removed after the war, Customs and Excise should show some elasticity; but " for any substantial addition to the national revenue," as the British Association Committee said in its 1916 report, " we should rely upon the Income Tax."

An Income Tax, if skilfully adjusted to the individual's ability to pay, is the fairest and most productive of taxes. It may be argued, indeed, that all other taxes are futile, except possibly those on a few articles in universal use which cannot be called necessaries, such as ꞁtobacco, or on things of which the consumption must in any case be regulated, such as intoxicants and motor spirit. Every one

9

has noticed how rises in the cost of living have been followed by successful demands for war bonuses or higher wages ; so that if the Chancellor of the Exchequer had tried to finance the war by taxes on commodities he would only have caused a further rise in wages and a further fall in the purchasing power of money.

It ought to be clear to every one that a man is not performing his duties as a citizen unless he pays his share of the national taxes. As Mr. Withers writes, in *Our Money and the State* (page 6) : " The citizen should under-stand about taxation, recognise it as good when it is good, and pay it cheerfully when it is equitable and well-distributed." A more famous author has said, " God loveth a cheerful giver ; "[1] it may even be argued that the command " Render unto Cæsar " asserts the duty of paying direct taxation. As it is there are now some twenty millions of electors, and perhaps three millions of Income Tax Payers ; so the old principle of " No taxation without representation " has been strangely turned round into " representation without taxation," or power without responsibility.

[1] 2 Corinthians IX. 7.

There is much force in Mr. Harold Cox's reply to. the National Expenditure Committee :[1] " I do not believe you will get any effective control over public expenditure until every elector has to pay a direct tax."

If the Income Tax is to yield more than it does now, and it will have to yield more than half as much again if the national accounts are to balance, it must be reformed. A second British Association Committee, of which I have the honour to be secretary, has been considering plans for " Income Tax Reform," but has not yet published a report, so I can only give my own proposals. Our chief difficulties have been (1) to decide at what point an income should be regarded as taxable, and (2) to frame an equitably graduated but flexible scale. My own scheme is as follows :

The highest point of total exemption seems to be fixed by the value of the pay and allowances received by the private soldier, since no one can feel himself unable to pay taxes if he is better off than a soldier. Mr. H. Samuel's Committee on National Expenditure estimates the total pay and allowances of a

[1] 121, 1918, page 25]

soldier at 40s. 6d. a week. This includes
married men and their families, so we may
take the figure for an unmarried soldier at
something between £50 and £70 a year.
Another criterion is the statuary minimum
wage recently fixed by Parliament for agricultural labourers, which is only 25s. a week.
Since this is obviously intended as the wage
of married men, it gives us a lower figure than
the soldiers' pay and allowances ; in fact it
appears so low that the rates fixed for particular counties are considerably higher, and
may average 30s. to 35s. These two criteria
seem to suggest that single men (or women)
should begin to pay Income Tax when their
income exceeds £60 a year, and married men
with families when their income exceeds £120
a year.

Under the existing scale (as fixed by Mr.
McKenna in 1915) no income is liable to tax
until it passes the £130 point, and then there
are allowances in respect of children, wife,
and dependents, at the rate of " the tax on
£25 " in respect of each. So the normal
citizen, who may be taken as a married man
with three children, gets first an abatement of
£120, and then an allowance of " the tax on

£25 " in respect of his wife and each of his three children if under sixteen. So he does not become a taxpayer until his income passes the £220 point, or more than double the average pay and allowances of the private soldier, whose job he may have taken. It has always seemed to me extraordinary during such a war, when we have compelled most, but not all, of our able-bodied men to fight, that every one who is for any reason exempt from military service does not exclaim : " Here, I want to do my bit ; put me down on the Income Tax Roll."

Personally, I share Mr. Harold Cox's view that *all* income ought to pay some rate of tax during war ; but no doubt this is a counsel of perfection, which will be impossible until the country has had more education in the duties of citizenship. On no intelligible basis, however, can it be contended that the man or woman who has over £75 a year, and no one else to support, ought not to pay Income Tax. Let us then take £75 a year as the starting-point. The real difficulty is to construct a graduated scale that will not destroy that most cherished device of Somerset House— " collection at the source "—which demands a standard rate, and not one which rises with every hundred pounds or so of income. At the same time, it seems absurd to deduct 6s. in the pound from all payments of what is called " unearned income," though it might just as well be called " income from savings," when most persons are only liable to pay 3s. or 3s. 9d. and have to claim repayment.

Is it possible to preserve collection at the source, and even to extend it, while making the tax easier to assess and collect, and fairer as between one taxpayer and another ? My plan which is described in *The Accountant* of June 8th, 1918, aims at fulfilling these three conditions. It divides Income Tax Payers into two great parties—those with less and those with more than £500 a year. A sub-division of the second class may be made of those below and those above £1,000 a year. Having laid down these two rules, I suggest the following plan :

(1) Tax the first £500 of all incomes at the uniform rate of 4s. in the pound.

(2) Tax the next £500 of all incomes at the uniform rate of 6s. in the pound.

(3) Apply the super tax (in form, but not in name) to all incomes above £1,000.

(4) Give an abatement of £75 to all incomes without limit.

(5) Give an allowance of the tax on £50, or on 10 per cent of the income, to all married men, with or without a maximum of, say, £200 a year.

(6) Give an allowance of the tax on £25, or on 5 per cent of the income, for each *bona fide* dependent of the taxpayer, with a maximum of £100 a year.

(7) If Differentiation is to be retained, give an allowance of one-fifth of the tax on all " earned " incomes.

Whether " 'differentiation " should be retained is a question of political expediency rather than of principle, and since it appears to favour the majority of electors at the expense of the minority, it is too much to expect that any Government will reverse the present rule. As a matter of fact the existing distinction between " earned " and " unearned " is an arbitrary one, and has much less historical support than the earlier distinction between " permanent " and " precarious " incomes.

Experience during the war, which has stopped or cut down " unearned " income from so many sources and has reduced the real value or purchasing power of all " unearned " income, suggests that salaries, especially those which are followed by pensions on retirement, are really less precarious than the income which is taxed at a higher rate. From the economist's point of view, the source of the taxpayer's income is of less importance than the claims upon it ; there can be no justification of a system under which a bachelor earning £900 a year pays £135, while a widow with the same income and three young children pays £168 15s. ; but for purposes of illustration I have suggested an " earned " rate one-fifth lower than the " unearned " rate. The following table shows the allowance which would be paid by M., a married man with three children, and by B., a bachelor without dependence :

Income. £			Married pays £			Bachelor pays £
150	.	.	Nil	.	.	15
200	.	.	Nil	.	.	25
300	.	.	20	.	.	45
450	`	.	50	.	.	75
600	.	.	85	.	.	115
1,000	.	.	185	.	.	235
2,000	.	.	460	.	.	560
5,000	.	.	1,572·10	.	.	1,672·10
10,000	.	.	3,697·10	.	.	3,797·10

This table gives the " unearned " rate ; if the " earned " rates be required it can be obtained by deducting one-fifth from the above figures. Under the ⁄Budget scale for 1918–19, M. and B. would pay as follows :

	Married pays.		Bachelor pays.	
Income.	"Earned."	"Unearned."	"Earned."	"Unearned."
	£ s. d.	£ s. d.	£ s. d.	£ s. d.
150 .	Nil	Nil	3 7 6·	4 10 0
200 .	Nil	Nil	9 0 0	12 0 0
300 .	9 0 0	12 0 0	20 5 0	27 0 0
400 .	28 0 0	37 10 0	39 7 6	52 10 0
600 .	60 0 0	75 0 0	75 0 0	93 15 0
1,000 .	150 0 0	187 10 0	150 0 0	187 10 0
2,000 .	450 0 0	525 0 0	450 0 0	525 0 0
5,000 .	1,787 10 0	1,787 10 0	1,787 10 0	1,787 10 0
10,000 .	4,187 10 0	4,187 10 0	4,187 10 0	4,187 10 0

The chief practical difficulty occurs over the smaller incomes, and this is my reason for suggesting the broad distinction between over and under £500 a year. All salaries, wages, or other periodical payments should be paid less tax at the rate of 4s. in the pound, and where the salary or wages is the main or only source of the taxpayer's income an allowance at the rate of £57 a year should be made. Other allowances may either be made at the time of payment or obtained quarterly from the local Surveyor of Taxes.

Dividends, interest, and similar " unearned " payments should be paid less the tax payable on incomes between £500 and £1,000 a year. Thereby a great deal of the reclaiming involved in the present system will be avoided ; and this rate (6s. in my scale) will be that payable by all companies and other corporations.

Incomes above £1,000 may be treated as if they were subject to super tax, *i.e.* each person will be separately assessed and will pay such rate beyond 6s. in the pound as the total amount of his income may determine. A scale is easily constructed :

Income	Income		Tax payable.
£1,000 to	£2,000	.	6s. 6d. on second £1,000.
2,000 „	3,000	.	7s. on third £1,000.
3,000 „	4,000	.	7s. 6d. on fourth £1,000.
4,000 „	10,000	.	An extra 3d. for each additional £1,000.
10,000 „	40,000	.	An extra 3d. for each additional £5,000.
4,0000 „	100,000	.	An extra 3d. for each additional £10,000.
Above	£100,000	.	Maxim rate of 12s. 6d. in the £.

The advantages of a scale such as that described above are (1) that it gets rid of all the " jumps " in the present tax, and that

the progression moves evenly from the lowest
to the highest point ; (2) that it involves no
change in the existing machinery of the tax.
It is a mere accident that the amount selected
as the standard rate (6s.) happens to be the
rate recently adopted by the Chancellor of
the Exchequer, for my scale is elastic, and its
poundage can be moved upwards or down-
wards, according to the needs of the Treasury.

It should be noted that the reduction of the
limit of total exemption to £75, or some such
low figure, is an essential part of the scheme,
as I rely upon the revenue thus obtained from
individuals who have no one but themselves
to support in order to lessen the burden on
married taxpayers, who have families to bring
up or aged parents to support. The allowances, too, are intended to be given without
regard to the total amount of the taxpayer's
income, though a limit may be placed upon
the amount of each allowance. Single men
and women with £900 a year have ample
means for all necessary expenditure ; parents
with children to feed, clothe, and educate
find that £900 a year goes a very little way.

As an income increases the proportion of
necessary expenditure decreases, that is why

the rate of tax should be higher and the proportion of allowances smaller.

I have worked out a rough calculation of the revenue which this scale should bring in after the war, and find that the total is between £450,000,000 and £500,000,000 a year.

CHAPTER XIII

A PEACE BUDGET

LET us now see how our Peace Budget works out with an Income and Super Tax yielding £475 millions. For some months to come, possibly for a year or two, the Excess Profits Duty will continue to furnish revenue after it has ceased to apply to profits which are actually earned. On the other hand the interest on our advances to the Allies and Dominions cannot be expected to reach its normal total for several years. Perhaps we may set the yield from the expiring Duty against the unpaid interest from our Allies.

	£
Income and Super Tax . . .	475,000,000
Excess Profits and Interest on Loans to Allies and Dominions .	75,000,000
Customs	106,000,000
Excise	60,000,000
Estate Duties . . . ⅃	32,000,000
Other Revenue	42,000,000
	790,000,000
Additions to the Motor and other Licence Duties . . .	20,000,000
	810,000,000

This total gives a margin of £60 millions over the estimated expenditure of £750 millions, which appears ample, and it may prove that the yield of the reformed Income Tax has been under-estimated. It is difficult to reckon what revenue any given change in the Income Tax would produce, because there are no statistics of the incomes between any points except for the Super Tax class, *i.e.* the incomes above £3,000 a year. Elsewhere (*Common Sense*, April 13th, 1918), I have tried to calculate what proportion of the national income falls to the various classes by taking the allowances on incomes between £130 and £700 a year. But the results thus obtained were so absurd that it seemed better to take some assumed figure for the total income and to divide it among various classes by guess-work. Perhaps one may divide it thus, putting the total income at £3,205 millions :

Income.	Numbers.	Average Income. £	Totals. £
i. Under £75 p.a.	5,000,000	60	300,000,000
ii. £75 to £200	10,000,000	130	1,300,000,000
iii. £200 to £500	2,000,000	350	700,000,000
iv. £500 to £1,000	500,000	700	455,000,000
v. £1,000 to £3,000	100,000	1,500	150,000,000
vi. Above £3,000	35,000	8,500	300,000,000
Totals	17,685,000		3,205,000,000

In this calculation the supposed war-income of £3,600 millions is reduced by £395 millions, it being assumed that no private employer working in competition can afford to spend money so lavishly as a Government which borrows what it needs and has no profit and loss account to consider. It is possible, of course, that the national income may fall still lower ; but it seems more likely that wages will not return to their pre-war levels, nor will prices. If the efforts put forth during the war are maintained when our soldiers come back, it may prove that the national output will remain at a far higher level than in 1913 ; in that case both the real and the money income of the nation will be far higher than in the years before the war. Only by increased production can we really " pay off " the War Debt. As Sir Hugh Bell, President of the Economic Section of the British Association, writes in the *Contemporary Review* for July, 1918 : " There are only two ways of discharging a debt, the honest and the dishonest : the honest way consists in either earning more or spending less, and using the balance to extinguish the obligation."

How much these six classes could or would pay in Income Tax must also be a matter for conjecture ; but if we reckon on nothing from Class i, an average of eighteenpence in the pound from Class ii, and a rate rising to eight shillings and sixpence for the sixth class, we get the following result :

Class.	Income.	Virtual Rate of Tax.	Yield.
i.	£300,000,000	Nil	Nil
ii.	1,300,000,000	1s. 6d.	£97,500,000
iii.	700,000,000	3s.	105,000,000
iv.	455,000,000	4s. 6d.	102,375,000
v.	150,000,000	6s. 6d.	48,750,000
vi.	300,000,000	8s. 6d.	127,750,000
	3,205,000,000		481,375,000

Or one might divide the national income into four quarters of £800 millions each, thus :

			Yield
i.	Free of Tax .	. .	Nil
ii.	Tax 2s. in £ .	. .	£80,000,000
iii.	„ 4s. „	. .	160,000,000
iv.	„ 6s. „	. .	240,000,000
	£3,200,000,000 yields	.	480,000,000

Put in this way the taxation appears extremely light. If the national income exceeds

£3,000 million a year there ought to be no difficulty in getting about £500 millions in Income Tax, which is, after all, only one-sixth of the total. Surely one-sixth of a man's income is a small thing to pay for having come through the Great War on the winning side !

INDIRECT TAXATION

The real aim of the reform scheme just described is to put our national revenue system on a sound basis. No system of taxation can be sound, or in the long run productive, unless it is based upon the principle of " ability to pay." The fault of our existing system is that this canon receives too little recognition. If a man's income lies anywhere between £130 and £400 a year he is taxed pretty nearly according to his ability Below £130 a year he is taxed according to the size of his family. Above £700 a year he is taxed without any consideration for the claims upon his income.

Since my scheme proposes to extend the Income Tax to incomes at present exempt, it is only fair that some adjustment should be made. This may be done most easily by

10

sweeping away the Sugar Duty entirely, and lowering the Tea, Coffee, and Beer Duties to their 1915 level. If it is found that our Peace Budget produces a substantial surplus this surplus should go first to lowering the Tobacco Duty and then to sweeping away entirely all the small taxes. Naturally that disastrous experiment in making things cheaper by taxing them, *i.e.* the Land Values Duties of the 1909–10 Budget, should be allowed to pass into a merciful oblivion. ᵂ

Under such a scheme of taxation people who are really poor will pay nothing worth mentioning, just a few pence on their pound of tea to remind them that citizenship has its duties as well as its rights, and something on their beer and their tobacco if they can afford these humble luxuries. But every one above the poverty line should pay a direct tax ; nothing but a direct tax assessed according to the individual's income, after allowances for the claims upon it, can harmonise the precepts of equity with the demands of the Chancellor of the Exchequer.

CONCLUSION

The reader may have noticed that I do not rely upon the usual objections which have been urged against a Capital Levy, such as the check to thrift, the impossibility of a fair assessment, the damage to the national credit, or the mechanical difficulties of collecting it. These have all been set out convincingly elsewhere. My purpose is to show that the arguments relied upon to prove the equity of the proposal are baseless, and that the great " fact " put forward by the protagonists of the Levy, *i.e.* their assertion that " the propertied classes have been made richer by the war," is not only inaccurate, but the reverse of the truth.

INDEX

Printed in the United States
by Baker & Taylor Publisher Services